PINORMAN

Books by Richard Aldington

NOVELS:
Death of a Hero
The Colonel's Daughter
All Men Are Enemies
Women Must Work
Very Heaven
Seven Against Reeves
Rejected Guest
The Romance of Casanova

SHORT STORIES:
Roads to Glory
Soft Answers

POETRY:
A Dream in the Luxembourg
Complete Poems

BIOGRAPHY:
Voltaire
Wellington
Four English Portraits
The Strange Life of Charles Waterton
Portrait of a Genius, But . . .
Pinorman

ESSAYS:
French Studies and Reviews
Literary Studies and Reviews
D. H. Lawrence

ANTHOLOGIES:
Poetry of the English-Speaking World
Fifty Romance Lyric Poems
The Religion of Beauty

PINORMAN

Personal recollections of Norman Douglas,
Pino Orioli and Charles Prentice

By

RICHARD ALDINGTON

"Εἰπέ τις, Ἡράκλειτε . . ."

WILLIAM HEINEMANN LTD
MELBOURNE :: LONDON :: TORONTO

FIRST PUBLISHED 1954

PRINTED IN GREAT BRITAIN
AT THE WINDMILL PRESS
KINGSWOOD, SURREY

ILLUSTRATIONS

The following Illustrations are printed as a complete section, and will be found between pages 62 and 63 :

AUTHOR'S NOTE

In these pages I have told what I believe to be the truth and no more, keeping to the facts as I found them; in which I had the aid of old letters, indispensable pegs of Time as well as reminders and refreshers of memory. But who can be certain of the exact form of little events and episodes which happened from fourteen to twenty-three years ago? Above all when I try to record the actual words that people uttered I do not pretend to give them more than approximately, giving the gist of the thing said and (I hope) in the character of the speaker. The reader who compares my versions of Pino's stories with those in his two books will find differences, ranging from details to the whole structure. That is because these stories passed through various evolutionary stages, and I have tried always to give the version I heard from his own lips. I believe Pino wrote those books and that Norman Douglas re-wrote them, and in so doing "ham'd them up" as the actors say. For personal motives he cut what displeased him and wrote in prejudices and thoughts which were not Pino's; he substituted his own style for Pino's, and thereby deprived him of much of his individuality and nearly all his verve. Of course, many, perhaps most, people will prefer Norman Douglas's Pino to mine, but I prefer to give mine if only for the sake of a few friends who knew him too.

Please do not read this book as an attempted biography of Norman Douglas. It is nothing but notes and personal recollections of him and two of his friends at the time when I knew them; and the whole book is intended to give Douglas's future biographer some of those personal touches which some biographers value highly and others detest.

ACKNOWLEDGMENTS

The unpublished letters from Norman Douglas are printed here by special permission of his literary executor, Mr. Kenneth Macpherson.

Mrs. Lyn Adamson gave permission for the printing of the letters and extracts from letters written by Charles Prentice. Messrs. Chatto & Windus added their consent in the case of those letters which were written by Charles Prentice from their office as one of the firm.

Signor Carlo Zanotti gave permission for the unpublished letters written by Giuseppe Orioli.

Mr. Kenneth Macpherson, Messrs. Secker & Warburg, Messrs. Chatto & Windus gave permission for the various quotations from Norman Douglas's books.

Signor Carlo Zanotti and Messrs. Chatto & Windus gave permission for the quotations from Giuseppe Orioli's books.

Mrs. Frieda Lawrence gave permission for the quotations from *Aaron's Rod* and from the letter on page 196.

I am greatly obliged to them all for their kindness in allowing me to make use of these documents and quotations.

I HAD best begin these notes by explaining that *Pinorman* is a portmanteau word used by themselves and friends for Pino (Orioli) and Norman (Douglas). At the time I knew them best they were inseparable, and you can hardly write of one without the other, and we were close friends with Charles Prentice (of Chatto & Windus), who published all three of us. Without Charles any account of those days and meetings is incomplete— not that I am aiming at completeness or anything like a formal biography of Douglas. Far from it. The idea is to put down, as truthfully as I can, after the uproar and disgusts of the last decade, notes on these three which may be of some use to future biographers of Norman Douglas. They may turn out to be worthless, but I must say that in writing biographies I have found personal notes very valuable and have wished for more. And while the chances of a wandering life have left gaps in my surviving letters from Pino and Norman, I have fortunately preserved quite a number from Charles in which one or both of them are mentioned, with the exact dates one so easily forgets or misplaces.

They say that the islanders of Ceos were much praised for the excellent laws they set forth in the great days of Hellas. One of these laws decreed that all citizens, male and female, when they reached the age of sixty were to rejoice together at a State-provided welfare banquet, at

the end of which they were all quietly poisoned by some
potent narcotic, which we hope was painless. There
must have been a considerable emigration of middle-aged
Ceans, though if the law were made permissive instead of
mandatory and applicable at any age it is hard to see what
objections could be raised. But if that law had been in
force in modern Europe I should never have met Norman
Douglas, since, when I met him in January, 1931, he had
just passed his sixty-second birthday. My last surviving
letter from him is dated July, 1939. It was the Pinorman
period—and if in trying to recapture its memories I give
something too much of the *moi haïssible*, try to forgive
it for the sake of these others.

The 'literary world' is narrow and self-centred. In
the spring of 1913 I spent several weeks at Anacapri, was
asked to lunch at various villas—chiefly German—and
heard not a word of Norman Douglas, though by that
time he should surely have been a Capri 'character' and,
according to *Looking Back*, must have been living as close
as Positano at the time. It is one more indication,
however slight, that the original publication of *Siren
Land* had failed to reach its public. Coming back on leave
to London in 1917 I found what remained of the 'literary
world' in war-time much occupied with a new novel
called *South Wind* by Norman Douglas. I read it and was
delighted, perhaps more than I should have been if its
light-hearted fantasy, a hedonism and setting in a dream
island half-Capri, half-Monaco, had not been so complete
and welcome a contrast to the scenes and dismal ethics
from which I had temporarily escaped.

In those early days I still had the impulse to make the
acquaintance of new writers whose work I liked, not
having learned the lesson of prudence that it is better and
less disillusioning to revere and enjoy from a distance. In

answer to such questions as I asked I learned that Norman Douglas had been in the diplomatic service (I am pretty sure it was a friend in the Foreign Office who first lent me *South Wind*), that he had been Assistant Editor of *The English Review*, and was now living abroad, nobody quite knew where. How was it that I did not meet Douglas before 1931? Well, he was always abroad and I was much in England until 1928, and when I began going back to Italy I spent much more time in and about Rome than in Capri or Florence, though I visited both. I now think that the breach between Douglas and Lawrence over *Aaron's Rod* and Magnus had never been healed on Douglas's side, and the fact that I stayed with the Lawrences at their farm near Florence did not recommend me to the pleader for better manners in literature.

As I shall tell later on, I had known Orioli slightly both as bookseller and member of the Italian Military Mission to England since about 1913, but I did not know of his intimate friendship with Douglas, and certainly had never seen the real Pino. Charles Prentice realised him much before I did, and urged me to see him whenever I was in Florence. I ought perhaps to interject here that in those happy days of the great 'depression' the earnings of a fairly successful literary man and a British passport enabled one to move happily about the civilised world with a freedom that is now reserved for Americans, the Aga Khan and the Duke of Windsor. This will explain to a generation of virtual prisoners what must seem an ostentation of travel—we lived travelling. I believe the freedom of these pre-1939 intellectual nomads stirred the bile of A. Hitler, who had never been out of Austria and Germany except as a prisoner of war, and he planned our destruction. Many of his ideas having been taken over by his alleged conquerors, we are where we are.

At all events I find a letter from Charles Prentice dated 18th November, 1929, which ends up:

"I am glad you are seeing Orioli, and I hope you will let me have any side lights you collect from him."

I remember very little of that encounter, for we were on our way to Sicily and Tunis, and spent only a few days in Florence. Pino was still shy and on the good behaviour which cramped his genius. But Charles's request to send him 'side lights' was certainly obeyed by me in the years to come, and if Chatto & Windus have not destroyed my letters to him they have a large collection of Piniana, not indeed publishable without judicious editing, but a cheerful set of anecdotes and sayings which ought to amuse posterity if posterity is ever allowed to have any fun, which looks unlikely.

There seems something very appropriate in the fact that I came to know Douglas partly for gastronomic reasons, or more exactly that the motive which took me to Florence in the winter of 1930–31 was a gastronomic one, though it was the pleasure of Pinorman's company which kept me there. In the autumn of 1930 I went from Venice to Brindisi by sea, and then on to Lecce, where I intended to stay until I had finished the book I was writing. I had long wanted to see Lecce; and its remoteness, especially in the winter months, guaranteed me from those callers and diversions which in more frequented places so fatally distract a writer from concentrated work. We had some idea of going on to Corfù for the rest of the winter after the book was finished.

Though Lecce is original and beautiful, an almost intact Baroque town preserved into the twentieth century, it had one disadvantage which I had not foreseen and against which nobody had warned me. In that out-of-season period of the year the cuisine of Lecce was meagre, not to say repulsive. B. and I became discouraged and eventually in low spirits from a series of disagreeable inadequate meals which in retrospect seem to have consisted always of chick-peas in greasy broth, tasteless boiled meat from which the broth had been made, spinach cooked in grease and sand, withered fruits, rancid cheese, and bread. The bread and wine were not bad, and if we could have foraged for ourselves I dare say we could have got by with spaghetti and olives and *provolone* and *tonno*. But none of these excellent things ever entered our menus. Quite unconsciously B. and I found that we were always talking of the kind of meals we should like if only we were somewhere else, as people are said to do when shipwrecked or otherwise threatened by starvation. An over-rationed generation will perhaps share our feelings of distress, and envy the ease with which we escaped.

When the book was finished there arose the question of where we should go. Corfù, as planned? I don't know why a memory ill-furnished from desultory reading brought up at that moment the remark of Lord Byron's valet, Fletcher, when his master went to Greece—his lordship, Fletcher exclaimed, must have been mad to leave Italy where they had everything for Greece where there was nothing to eat but tough nanny-goat and nothing to drink but turpentine. Clearly, Fletcher knew nothing of Puglia, and yet if we abandoned Lecce it seemed rather ridiculous to go north in December. It happened that Charles Prentice had been with us in Venice and had written from London the following account of his meeting with Douglas and Orioli in Florence on his way home:

"Douglas and Orioli were very full of life. We had a startling dinner. Grey truffles cooked with cheese in sizzling pannikins, the stench *dreadful* but the taste good, a licentious dish. Then a remarkable stew of jugged hare with an oriental-like sauce compounded of currants, pine-nuts and chocolate corrected with vinegar, a dish fit for the Caliph. And a paunch of white Chianti, rare and very special, that swung amorously in its shining cradle. Orioli enquired about Aretino,* but I gave him an evasive reply. He was most insistent that you should come to Florence and see Norman Douglas. But it was a quieter evening than the one in May, and after dinner we went to O's flat, played Brahms on the gramophone and looked at books." (Letter of 10th November, 1930.)

I think it must have been that letter which decided us to go back to Florence for a week or two, which eventually became several months.

There are points in that paragraph from Charles's letter which are well worth the attention of Douglas's future biographer for hints about Douglas's way of life as it appeared to his friends in Florence in the 1930s. He loved to take advantage of any event, a birthday, the arrival or departure of a friend, or a mere whim, to arrange a little feast such as Charles describes in his letter. As a rule Douglas refused to go to the tourist or hotel restaurants—those which appeared in Baedeker—though he did sometimes go to Picciolo's and Betti's and even to Baglioni's. He lived alone in his flat above Pino's on the Lungarno, and so far as I know always lunched and dined out at one of the smaller, almost peasant, places

* Pino wanted me to translate one of Aretino's comedies for his Lungarno Series. I did not want to give any more time to translating, and Charles defended me perfectly.

where he was sure to meet no English and American tourists, where he could order dishes to be prepared specially for his strange and exacting tastes, where he could get wine which was not always 'muck', where he could be perfectly free and at his ease, and where of course he was a known and privileged person. The one thing which displeased him, apart of course from a disappointing flask or a dish which failed, was that the waiters and *padroni* in these places tried to flatter him by calling him "Professore". It irritated him very much. How often he would say: "I wish to God they'd stop that damned Professore nonsense. Hanged if I'll ever go to that place again." But there were so few places which met his requirements that he always did go back, and of course they always went on calling him Professore. "Damn fools!"

In due course I was taken to the restaurant mentioned in Charles's letter. I have forgotten its name and even its address, though I remember it was a long way from the Lungarno where we all lived and probably somewhere near the Piazza Cavour. On the other hand, I have a fairly clear recollection of the proprietor-cook-waiter, who was called Sor Giovanni—'Sor' being the old Florentine colloquialism for 'Signor'. He was a dark, lean, close-cropped, wooden-featured peasant, who never smiled even at Pino's most uproarious jokes and funniest pantomime. Piqued, Pino nicknamed him Strindberg, and it was as Strindberg rather than as Sor Giovanni that we knew him. I find a reference to him in a letter to me from Pino:

"N. and I had a good dinner at Strindberg the other night, drunk a little much both of us. I went on burning Rothenstein book and all the crowd in it except Degas, Ingres and Renoir and Botticelli."

I have a hazy recollection that Sor Giovanni Strindberg came originally from the Abruzzi, but that he had spent a good many years as a cook in Austria. This, of course, would account for his being patronised by Norman, who, having been brought up in Vorarlberg, had an unfortunate liking for their chives-haunted dishes. That menu he and Pino gave Charles in November, 1930, would probably not be to everyone's taste as it certainly was not to mine. How well and unhappily do I remember those grey truffles in cheese! They did indeed, as Charles says, smell 'dreadful'. The effluvium to my perception was exactly that of acetylene gas, though I admit that if you survived the gas attack they tasted well enough. Reggie Turner, whom we all respected because he had stood by Oscar Wilde when all the world ratted, had a horror of these grey truffles. Flapping his eyelids like a demented owl, as Lawrence wickedly but exactly described him in *Aaron's Rod*, Reggie at the appearance of this dish would glance angrily at us, and particularly at Norman who had led us astray, and utter what he considered sparkling witticisms at our expense. Dear Reggie! they were so witty, and I can't remember one of them.

Norman was unmoved by these attacks, and defiant. "Ha! You can't put me off my food. Say anything you like. Go on. I don't care. There's only one thing can put me off, and you don't know it." In those days I used to wonder what it was. After the publication of *Looking Back* it seemed fairly clear that this emetic idea must be lobster boiled in Benedictine, which, as Norman tells us, he foolishly consumed on his twenty-first birthday feast, with the result that he was sick for days and the very smell of Benedictine always nauseated him. Must I confess that more than once when I heard him make that boast I thought of murmuring "lobster in Benedictine"? Was it

wholly cowardice which made me refrain? Think how
awful if it had been the one thing which did make him
nauseate his dinner! Pino would never have talked with
me again.

Fortunately, I was spared that jugged hare in Caliph
sauce. I have a memory that about the time I met Norman
he had become convinced that Florentine hares were all
cats, a prejudice which no argument could remove. We
offered to buy him a hare with its pads on and take it to the
restaurant. "Pah! they'll steal it for themselves, and serve
up the kitchen cat as usual." So we never had hare. But
I do remember going with him to Betti's to eat wild
boar done with that chocolate and vinegar sauce, as
it is everywhere in Italy, the recipe for which Norman
has printed as if he were Columbus discovering America.
Anyway, wild boar, though romantic-sounding, is such
tasteless game that it needs some strenuous addition.
I remember thinking of the perfection with which
venison and marcassin are served in France, and marvelling that Norman really preferred these pungent
barbarities.

That 'paunch of white Chianti' with the jugged hare
brings up another aspect of Norman's tastes. What would
be the correct drink with those incandescent truffles of
his I can't imagine—vodka or vitriol, I should think—
but I must say that the serving of a white wine with so
pungent a dish seems to be a blunder. With that chocolate
and vinegar sauce and the heavy boar's flesh a delicate old
white Chianti must have been completely obliterated—
it should have been served with oysters, followed by sole
or red mullet, and cheese straws. But with that Sor
Giovanni menu you might as well have gone the whole
hog—start with cocktails and smoke thoughout the meal.
With a highly over-flavoured dish like the wild boar and

chocolate-vinegar there was nothing to do but to serve the heaviest and oldest red wine available—a Montepulciano or a rich old red Chianti. But no! That would have been 'too strong', for the simple reason that Norman cared nothing about having the right type of wine. What he wanted was to drink out a couple of flasks of light wine —and never mind the menu!

He had the most strange ideas of what made up a harmonised menu, and though I applauded his independence, I sometimes ate his meals with disrelish. The very last time I (Dutch) lunched with him—1938—he arranged to meet me at the Café de Paris at Cannes. Now—damn it!—you don't go to a great restaurant like that to eat spaghetti followed by boiled chicken and rice *et un vin quelconque*, but I vow to God that is what he had ordered for us. He may have been on a diet, of course; in which case he should have ordered for himself, and left his friends to choose something a little less primitive. The fact is that Norman's culinary taste had been formed on provincial Austria, Scotland and London, and he had little knowledge of higher things. His sojourns in France had been brief and often penniless, and he had never perlustrated the regions of Burgundy and Bordeaux with veneration. I invited him once to the best restaurant (of the day) in St. Raphael, where both the *maître d'hôtel* and *sommelier* were friends and allies. I drove over the day before to explain (*avec des billets de banque, quoi!*) that I wished to honour *un homme de lettres, un poète* . . . Instantly, they were alert, and soon blocked me out a good menu and sequence of wines, which I knew were authentic and such as money can seldom buy outside of France. Will it be credited? As I came back from paying the bill in the background I found that Norman had ordered for himself a portion of that worst of all Italian

cheeses, Bel Paese, and a bottle of *vin ordinaire! Il aspira
à descendre!*

But in my story I have not yet even met Douglas, so that
this talk of restaurants and menus may seem premature and
irrelevant. But that future biographer, if he has kept his
eyes open, will have seen whither this is tending. In this
daily *terre-à-terre* matter of feeding, Norman was a strong
individualist, not caring much about others so long as he
got what he wanted himself. No food and wine snob, he
had considerable pretensions to a critical taste in such
things though it was far indeed from the classic taste he
thought to uphold in literature. Moreover, the luncheon
or dinner table was his favourite meeting place. He rarely
asked anyone to his flat under the eaves, though he sometimes joined us in Pino's flat, and in mine when for some
months I rented one in Piazza Santa Croce. He liked company at table, and we lunched or dined with him almost
daily at one or other of the little restaurants he frequented
—the Nuova Toscana, Bianca, and Fusi are those I
remember best. Now, though the proprietors were no
doubt flattered to have him as a regular customer, the
trouble was he expected more than they could provide
at so low a price. Consequently he was often disappointed,
and his letters abound with complaints of the 'muck' he
was forced to eat and drink in Florence.

It was much the same with those cheap Toscano cigars
he used to smoke, or try to smoke, on the theory that
they were the purest tobacco in Italy. Perhaps they were,
but they certainly were among the strongest, and their
odour was not of Havana, although I got to like them in
time. There was tragi-comedy in the spectacle of Douglas
trying to find an after-luncheon or dinner Toscano which
would draw properly, for they were usually screwed up so
tightly—like tobacco twist—that no air could be drawn

through them. He invariably carried half a dozen or so in an upper pocket. One by one he would pick them out, try to light them, find they would not draw, and throw each in turn on the tablecloth with an impatient "Pah!", going off into some whimsically exaggerated denunciation of the Italian State tobacco monopoly. Defeat was recognised when at last he reluctantly cut or broke one of the cigars in half (in which state they would draw), since, for some reason I never discovered, they were supposed to be perfect only if smoked whole, though I must say that the Italian cigar connoisseurs I observed, such as cabmen, peasants and porters, invariably smoked halves. At such moments Douglas often reminded me of the man in Huysmans's *A Vau-l'eau*, who spent a life of bitterly frustrated hopes trying to buy a louis dinner for a crown. It was so much a matter of dogma with Norman that he could walk all round any Italian without getting out of his chair that he was always attempting the impossible in restaurants.

The Ristorante Bianca I mentioned was in a turning off Via Porta Rossa, just before you get to Via Tornabuoni. It was convenient for me when I was living at the Gran Bretagna, since it gave a few minutes' walk and a breath of fresh air between work and lunch. I think it was not in any of the guide books, and except for ourselves there were only Italians. We had been introduced there by Pino as personal friends of his, so escaped that unpleasant mingling of intrusive familiarity and swindling with which too many restaurateurs of those days hoped to stimulate the foreign tourist trade. In winter the Bianca had a speciality which reminded me of Simpson's in London where they used to bring round large roasts on a trolley. The Bianca trolley was loaded with boiled meats—boiled tongue, boiled beef, boiled pork, boiled fowls, on one occasion a boiled turkey, and always a huge boiled sausage. Certainly it was heavy diet, but after Lecce and on a cold winter day very acceptable. I think it was this trolley load of *bolliti* and *lessi* which attracted Douglas.

Evidently Norman was not in Florence when we arrived somewhere about Christmas, 1930, for I find a letter from Charles which says:

"B. is quite right to take you on to Florence. I am afraid, though, that you miss Douglas again, for I have just heard from him to the effect that he has to be in Paris about the 10th—the poor fellow has got to go into a nursing home and have all his teeth out, recover, and be fitted with new ones. What dreadfully bad luck. Orioli, however, I gather will still be on the Lung'arno, cursing the dilatoriness of his printers, though Douglas says he is trying to get him to join him in Paris later on. But you will know of all this long before you get my letter." (4th December, 1930)

But Orioli certainly did not go to Paris, for a letter of the 15th December says:

"I rejoice that Orioli has been so friendly, and that you are so comfortably installed. I would give you a message for him, were I not writing to him myself to thank him with N.D. for *Paneros*. I wonder if he is going on to Paris. It is too unfortunate your missing Douglas again, and I don't suppose you will be staying in Florence so very long . . ."

I complete this series of extracts from Charles's letters on this topic with a sentence from one dated the 28th December, 1930, and written from his home in Scotland:

"The office also sent on a letter from Douglas, which rejoiced me greatly, saying that he was returning at once to Florence, and hoping that he'd catch you before you were off again."

Pino had given us some warning that Douglas would join us for lunch next day at Bianca. We had just sat down and were looking over the menu when a tall, powerfully-built, white-haired man came into the restaurant, glanced quickly round, and then made for our table. He introduced himself as Norman Douglas, apologised lightly for 'intruding', and asked if he might sit at our table. As if he needed to ask! I was attracted by the neatness and exquisite cleanliness of his person—an aristocratic refinement of toilet—and by his manners. No plebeian ever achieves that seemingly effortless courtesy which puts one instantly at ease without the slightest trace of condescension. And yet the meeting was unconventional and bohemian, and the place a restaurant for commercial travellers, *contadini* and tradesmen of the quarter. I don't know whether other people just met Douglas in so casual a manner, but this one seems to me so characteristic that it was worth recording. Whatever may have been the case in his diplomatic and opulent days, he had unquestionably come to dislike formal gatherings, meetings and introductions. He guarded his personal liberty most carefully, and hated to waste a minute of life on anything or anybody he found tedious. From the remarks in Charles's letters I infer that he and Pino had given us a good character, but obviously Norman meant to try us out before allowing any intimacy. A prepared 'accidental' meeting in a tavern carried no social obligations. If he found us bores or uncongenial, how easy to talk for a few minutes and then courteously 'evaporate' (as he could so expertly) to

another restaurant, and thereafter take good care not to
see us again! It was no doubt a technique perfected after
much experience, but on this occasion he did not use it.
If I am not deceived we sat on talking at the Bianca until
nearly four o'clock.

At that date Norman Douglas had just passed his sixty-
second birthday. He was tall, heavily built without being
fat, moving with the stiffness of age, but always straight-
backed and dignified, walking always with a stick and the
unhurried tireless stride of a mountaineer. From a
distance, and especially from the rear view, he looked very
Scottish. How Scottish his face was I only realised from
one of Pino's tricks. When we were in Sicily together
Pino and I bought up in a remote village its entire stock of
the most atrociously gaudy tam-o'-shanters ever seen in a
nightmare, which we designed for the members of our
secret conspiracy, the C.L.S. One afternoon Norman was
placidly smoking a pipe when Pino clapped one of these
bonnets on his head, and fell back to contemplate the
result.

"My gawd!" said Pino awe-struck, "vot a Scawtch is
Norman!"

It was true. As he sat there, unmoved, in that parody
of his native bonnet, he looked as Scotch as a Lowland
laird enjoying a godly lecture on eternal damnation in the
kirk on a misty Sabbath.

But that first day at the Bianca he did not seem particularly Scotch to me, and he certainly had no trace either
of Scottish or German accent. Nor for the matter of that
was it any noticeable English accent. His features were no
longer handsome, though you saw he must have been very
handsome in youth, but they were clearly marked. His
nose was large and prominent but well-shaped, his lips
well-formed and firm, the line of his jaw and chin full of

power, his ears set close to his head, and his comely white hair still parted in the middle as it had been since he was a schoolboy at the Karlsruhe Gymnasium. His eyes, though lacking the strange beauty of our friend Lawrence's, were very expressive, especially in so old a man, and enlivened his whole face to animation when he was amused or interested or indignant. The coloured drawing of Norman Douglas by his friend Otto Sohn-Rethel gives a startlingly true likeness of his appearance in the 1930s. It gives his features exactly; and also his red complexion and the dissipated look which made the puritan Lawrence describe his face as that of 'a fallen angel'. (What next!) But that Sohn-Rethel sketch also preserves a curiously unhappy expression which was habitual to Douglas's face in repose, above all when he thought he was not observed. It was a look of suffering as well as of discontent.

"Everyone complains of his memory, but nobody of his intelligence." At this moment I might legitimately complain of both, for I omitted to make notes of any meetings and talks with Douglas, and have only memories which I know to be uncertain and fallible. Boswellising was never in my line, and a wandering writer travels light and burdens himself with no superfluous papers. By a good luck I don't deserve I have found a few scraps of letters from Douglas and Orioli between the leaves of Charles Prentice's letters which had to be kept for 'business' reasons. Among them I have found a record of that lunch which I had quite forgotten.

Some excellent prawns, which had been saved for him, put him in a good humour, and the cradled wine-flask was often tilted. Somebody suggested potato salad with the prawns. "I'll make it for you." This was a lucky stroke, for within his own limits Norman was a good cook. I can see him now with the chopped potatoes, the oil and other condiments, and above all the chopped chives, Austrian-fashion, his glasses on his nose, discoursing as he fabricated an excellent salad. I wish I could remember what he said, but it has all gone.

The 'relic' of this meeting, so strangely preserved, is a piece of folded paper (probably supplied by the restaurant) on which Douglas has written two specimens of ancient German poetry. The first reads:

> Es traumete Kriemhilden
> In Tugender der sie pflac
> Das sie einen Valken wilden
> Zügge maneggan Tac
> Den ihr zwo Arn erkrummen
> Da—? sie des mnosste sehen
> Ihr enkunde in dirre Welte
> Leider nimmer syn geschehen.

This must be a fragment of the *Nibelungenlied*. The other sounds more like a snatch from a Minnesinger:

> Ich hiort ein Wasser diessen
> Und sach die Vische fliessen,
> Ich sach, swas in der Werlte was
> Veld oder Wald, Laub, Baum und Gras.

I think the word in the last line must be 'Laub' though in Norman's hasty scribble it looks like 'Land'. How on earth did I come to preserve this? I think I must previously have picked up my letters from Cook's (which was close at hand) and that on leaving I pushed this piece of paper into the envelope containing a letter from Charles where long afterwards I found it. But how on earth did we get on to ancient German poetry? It is true that B. knew German, having been brought up by German governesses, so it must have been for her benefit. And he may have written it down for me, as I could not understand it when spoken. Douglas was bi-lingual, German being as much his mother tongue as English—he had a German or Austrian grandparent on his mother's side and was brought up chiefly in Austria and Germany. Frieda Lawrence, who is wholly German, always maintained that Norman was wittier and more amusing in German than he was in English.

It is rather a shot in the dark, but I think we may have got on to this primitive German verse by way of our friend, C. K. Scott-Moncrieff, who had translated *Beowulf* and the *Chanson de Roland*. I think Norman may have scribbled those lines to show me that Germany also had an ancient poetry, though it is obviously absurd to suppose that the *Nibelungenlied* has the antiquity of *Beowulf* and the *Volsunga Saga*. But how had we got on to Scott-Moncrieff, who somewhere about that time had died of cancer in Rome? Scott-Moncrieff was an ardent convert to Roman Catholicism, and Norman Douglas an equally ardent critic of that faith. Both in print and speech Norman was nothing if not outspoken in his criticism of Christianity—combining, I used to think, the amused curiosity of a scientist, the cheerful contempt of an Epicurean philosopher and a touch of that old Presbyterian zeal. I suppose the Scottish clannishness triumphed over all these difficulties, for Norman (like myself) certainly visited the dying man in a Roman hospital managed by nuns. By way of epitaph on our friend Norman made this disquieting remark: "Of course in that damned Roman Catholic place they didn't give him enough morphia."

If this seems a meagre harvest from such a first meeting, I can only plead that it is better than remembering more than was said and done.

My next Douglas scrap is written by him on the note-paper of my hotel, the Gran Bretagna:

Sunday

12.50

Dear Aldington,

Such a charming notice of Paneros in the Referee—ever so many thanks!

I dine at *Picciolos*, near Piazza Cavour, at about 8. Do come if you can with B., to whom best love.

Yours ever

Norman Douglas

I wish this brought up something in the way of memories, but I can't remember whether we made up for missing him at lunch by dining with him at Picciolo's. Picciolo! I have forgotten even the place, except that it seems to have been rather large, with that austerity of aspect peculiar to Italian restaurants of the cheaper kind. All told during those months in Florence I received dozens more of such messages, but all have been lost save one. The tone of this shows that it must date from a later period, but probably still 1931. It is written on the notepaper of the Ristorante Nuova Toscana:

"2.30

Dear Richd,

Just missed you; but read your English newspaper. I dine to-night at Bianca. Anything for a change (of environment: the muck they give you is everywhere the same.)

Yours

N.D."

Such a scrap is not worth publishing, except for the

confirmation it brings to what I was saying before about his perpetual efforts to get a twenty-francs (gold) meal for five francs, and lamentations over the 'muck' he was forced to eat. Such things are always relative. To the appetite of a man nearly twenty-five years younger than himself the fare of those restaurants Norman abused so heartily was acceptable enough, if one kept in mind the inevitable limitations of cheap restaurants and did not forget the privations of Lecce, with which after all Douglas was far better acquainted than we were from his many wanderings in South Italy. If you wanted greater luxury and variety, Florence could supply them, but they had to be paid for—and it was not so easy there to walk round the proprietors without getting out of your chair.

Equally characteristic were the notes—of which I have preserved none—sent over by the hand of one of his friends among the street urchins, or left by himself, with some such warning as this: "Don't forget. Fusi at 8 sharp. Pino insists they have *abbacchio*, which he has ordered." *Abbacchio*, of course, is spring lamb; and what Norman liked—indeed insisted on—is that we should club together to order a whole fore-quarter or hind-quarter to be roasted at Fusi's, which is not as piggy as it sounds since they were very small. When the moment came he loved to take charge of the carving, for then he could cut himself the morsels he liked best, and not be at the mercy of the restaurant. The assertion in his note that Pino had 'insisted' on lamb and had 'ordered' it was one of his fictions. Most likely Pino would have preferred to invite us all to dine quietly with him in his flat, where he was well looked after by an old peasant woman, the mother of his assistant, Carletto. Pino's hankering after spring lamb was a convenient myth.

Usually Pino was as yielding as plasticine under

Norman's dominant will, but at one of these *abbacchio* feasts he rebelled memorably. Norman had begun by saying when the joint was brought: "Don't let that damned waiter touch it—he'll mangle it and keep all the best for himself. Here, I'll carve it for you." He had then handsomely given us what he didn't want himself, and having carved out the morsels he did want had slyly helped himself to both the kidneys. Pino at that moment was drinking wine, but on perceiving this invasion of our just rights was overcome with indignation. Putting down his glass, and hastily and rather noisily wiping a wet mouth on the back of his hand to save time, he sprang to his feet, pointed a denunciatory finger—Cicero at Cataline—and declaimed:

"Look at him! Because he have written *Sous Wind* he is a great man and steal our kidney!"

I never heard a better exposure of tyranny.

2

I STILL have my copy of the original issue of *Paneros*, number five in the Lungarno Series, limited to 250 copies. It was priced at three guineas, a stiff price for an essay of about 15,000 words somehow stretched out to 160 pages. This was the equivalent of six or seven guineas today, and could only have been justified if the contents had been a literary masterpiece and the production a splendid example of modern printing and binding. I don't think *Paneros* was either of these. Perhaps it was prejudice—but I don't think so, for I was very ready to admire—but I never could get up much enthusiasm for the Lungarno Series books from the point of view of book-production. True, they were unprentious and without æsthetic frills, but they seemed quite without charm and far inferior to such so-called 'commercial' books as those designed by Charles for Chatto's at a quarter the price. The Lungarno Series type was legible but dull; the paper solid but yellowish; the binding too thick and heavy. Douglas's *Capri Materials*, though only 350 pages, is a very unwieldy book.

I have often wondered how far Douglas's taste influenced his Lungarno publications. Considering how easily Pino was influenced by him, I should think it quite likely that they embodied Douglas's ideas. There was a solid clumsiness which reminds me of Norman's winter clothes, which were made of good Scottish tweed sadly bungled by a back-street Italian tailor. In both cases the aim was evidently for solidity and sober good taste, but I rather doubt whether Norman or Pino had enough practical experience to succeed in the very difficult art of fine printing. Nor do I think Norman really understood the limitations of a small press. I can give an example of this, which at the time left me dumbfounded. A well-off friend of ours, whom I will call K., had started a hand-press for no particular reason, and Norman and I had both been laid under contribution. One day there arrived a 'book' made up—let us say—of a story by Galsworthy. It wasn't Galsworthy, but another very popular author of the time. Norman picked this up from my table, peered at it through his glasses with some distaste, and began to denounce its uselessness. What, he asked, was the point of putting out a couple of hundred copies of a work by a man whose books sold twenty or thirty thousand, none of whose readers in all probability collected 'Press' books? The production must have been a nuisance to Galsworthy and to his English and American publishers by delaying the main publication. So far this was all Norman's customary good sense, and I agreed completely. But to my astonishment he then proceeded:

"Now, instead of wasting time and materials on modern stuff like this, why on earth doesn't K. bring out a complete Athenæus with a translation and plenty of notes, scholarly stuff?"

I didn't know what to say. Of course such an edition of Athenæus was most desirable, but was K. with his one-man hand-press the right and practical means of producing it? So far as I know, K. had not the slightest interest in Greek literature and I dare say didn't even know the Greek alphabet. The Loeb Athenæus with Dr. Gulick's trans-lation now fills seven volumes of about 400 pages each, and the notes are cut to a strict minimum. Supposing you could find the scholarly commentator, how many hundreds of extra pages would be needed for notes on all the innumerable topics started by Athenæus, and how many decades would K. have had to labour at his press to get it all printed? There are certainly some limitations resulting from the gentlemanly life. One was that Norman found it news when I told him the Loeb Series was publishing Athenæus.

I have been looking over this essay of Norman's after the lapse of years, and wondering who paid that price for it. *Paneros*—which Pino insisted on pronouncing 'Paneeross' in the style of the B.B.C.—is the fabulous gem 'All-Love', said to have been described by a philosopher of antiquity, thus hinting at Douglas's topic of aphrodisiacs and the preservation of sexual energy. In spite of this promising theme the book contrives to bring together several elements of unpopularity. It reads like an appendix or very long footnote to Burton's *Anatomy* tricked out in the sententious style of Sir Thomas Browne, without the don's raciness or the doctor's majesty. It is filled with fantastic and obsolete quackeries culled from forgotten medical writers of long ago. There are whole pages of quoted medical Latin, whole paragraphs in English which are merely catalogues of superstitious drugs. The author has obviously read the notes to Sir Richard Burton's *Arabian Nights* and knows something of modern medical science.

It is hard to see *Paneros* as anything but another of Douglas's too obvious efforts at book-making. Some critics have gone so far as to call it 'sterile antiquarianism', a charge which cannot be wholly brushed off. Certainly, he no more believed in the aphrodisiacs of his defunct and forgotten savants than he believed in the miracles of Suor

Serafina de Dio. His Scotch atheism, in which he outdid
David Hume, was at once amazed and amused by the
fantastic absurdities of these forgotten writers. Douglas
had the virtuoso's and the schoolboy's serious rapture over
freaks. His native Vorarlberg bred and piously preserved,
to the Greater Glory of God, astonishing idiots known
locally as *Dorftrottels*, who had fascinated Douglas from
childhood. Suor Serafina and the grotesque medicine
men quoted in *Paneros* were for him a kind of *Dorftrottels*
of the intelligence—mental freaks worth studying. His
stark Scotch rationalism, which was not wholly exempt
from superstition, delighted in their extravagances.

Where did he find the texts of these 'scholarly aridities',
this 'assemblage of empirical divagations and delusions'?
He and Pino tried to make a mystery of it, but there is not
the slightest doubt that he found them in Pino's own book-
shelves—the firm of Davis and Orioli, Libraria Antiquaria,
specialised in rare and ancient medical works.

This pedestrian compilation of learned trifles is enlivened
by poignant sentences—delight in sensual desire, regret
for Youth's passing, rebellion against Death, disdain for
those who waste the golden years hunting a delusive after-
life. This bookish pedant, rejoicing in the learned
nonsense of Pino's antiquarian medical trash, is also a
wistful hedonist, passionate, a voluptuary:

"Why prolong life save to prolong pleasure? What
pleasures are comparable to those of youth? And what
ecstasy, of all of them, is more fervid than that of young
lovers locked in voluptuous embracement, beside
which every other joy of earth sinks to the consequence
of a trifle . . .?"

But then of course comes the other side of the picture.

There is the inevitable Death, "a torment, a terror, a wintry thing, which comes to hug us to its body and drag us underground, away from friends and sunshine, into that uncomfortable night of nothing; there to rot like any carrion dog."

Hence the deluded search for an Elixir of Youth which would make desire immortal; or, since that is obviously hopeless, the search for an Elixir of Sex to prolong for however short a time that 'fervid ecstasy', in which Douglas has some hope. At best the perfect aphrodisiac would be a mere reprieve, for if there were no Death there would be no Sex. The Hellenic myth-makers were inconsequent when they mated immortal gods and goddesses to over-populate Olympus. Living bodies transmit life because they must lose it, and Douglas's hopes of prolonging Desire artificially are a delusion. Perhaps he might have lifted his druggists and jugglers to something more than murky antiquarian freaks by linking them to that most ancient Life Quest which lurks behind all Magic and Religion, but he knew nothing of it.

Very likely I am being too serious about a little book which was intended as a learned jest, and yet I can't help thinking that Norman missed an opportunity to develop some of the ideas suggested by his theme. How admirably he might have discoursed on the myth of the immortality of the soul in all its various forms from Osiris to Mrs. Blavatsky! He might have told us much about that naif and cynical 'religion' of the South which without troubling about ethics or spirituality takes a lottery ticket in the Catholic Church which may win the prize of Heaven— and if it doesn't? Well, 'Faith' hasn't been allowed to interfere with the pleasures of life on earth, so where's the complaint? And I wish he might have diverged from that to a topic he ought to have treated and never did, namely, why 'superstition' has produced so many admirable creations, from basilicas to illuminated MSS, from plain-song to cordial liqueurs, from Romanesque sculpture to miracle plays, from cloisters to chivalry, while impeccable Lowland Scotch rationalism has never produced anything which could give pleasure to anyone. . . .

But I think I can guess why *Paneros* remained an undeveloped sketch which, in spite of its literary skill, reads too often like a painful task. Even at the best of times writing was a task for Douglas, and by the time he came to *Paneros* he was sixty and had lost whatever pleasure in writing he may have had in earlier years. Writing had become an affliction, even for a Scottish gentleman-amateur who wrote only for money. It must have needed all Pino's powers of persuasion and the hope of sharing in those guineas to make him finish the dreary task. Whoever invented that portmanteau 'Pinorman' expressed a truth, for without Pino would Norman have had the spirits to do any more writing or the energy to print and distribute his books? Pino was the link between us all, for if Norman naturally preferred him to Charles and me, we preferred him as a person to Norman, no matter how much we respected Norman as a great writer.

Somewhere or other, in his donnish way, Walter Pater attributes 'blitheness' to the ancient Greeks as one of their distinguishing characteristics. If so, in that respect Pino was an ancient Greek born out of his due time. He was as blithe a spirit as Shelley's skylark, and blither too. He was inexhaustibly cheerful. I don't know where we get the word 'skylarking', but he was up to that too. I have never known a more admirable companion. D'Annunzio says somewhere that Italians are 'sad sensualists'. Well, Pino wasn't that sort of Italian. Everything he touched turned to mirth. He never allowed life to go trite and stale, he was always observant and amused, and kept one up to his level. After D. H. Lawrence, a long way after, Pino had a keener sense of life than any man I have known.

I used to watch him sometimes from behind my curtain as he crossed Piazza Santa Croce. Instead of hurrying along unseeingly or lounging indifferently, like the other people in the square, he strolled with a jaunty step, constantly turning his head from one side to the other, noticing every detail of the little street scenes which are constantly going on in Florence, stopping to listen to a group of men arguing, pushing off at a tangent to investigate something which had caught his attention. And when the door-bell had rung and he was let in, ten to one he would begin:

"What do you sink I see as I am coming along . . .?"

Like so many Italians, he was a natural actor, doubled by a natural story-teller of genius, but you must not suppose that he had anything in common with the usual dining-out *raconteur* or the licensed mimic. As a mimic he was much inferior to Lawrence, who was at once deadly satirical and endlessly amusing—a 'born copy-cat', as David Garnett says. Pino took a scene from life or from something he had imagined and re-acted it for you with all the embellishments of a vivid fancy. I used to call him Boccaccio junior and Norman the Old Pretender. Frieda Lawrence had the same thought. She had sat once very quiet in Pino's book-shop listening as he talked to an enthralled audience of Italians about some mountain he had climbed; and, said Frieda, he made the country seem so far away and the mountains so high and the things he and Norman did so wonderful—it was like Boccaccio.

In English these tales or recitals or re-enactments had a special touch of fantasy and unexpectedness, due to Pino's personal views on the syntax and pronunciation of English. In the same way his English spelling gave a special flavour to his letters. Unluckily a gift like this cannot be transmitted beyond the immediate audience. It is always hard to catch laughter in a net of words, and Pino as a writer is far below Pino as an actor story-teller. Most of the stories in his two books are ruined by 'style' or reduced to the ordinary by having all the zest and special quality taken out of them. Partly perhaps this is due to the fact that his everyday Muse freely indulged in a vocabulary which is very seldom printed. But the real reason is that Norman re-wrote the books in his own style, imposing on Pino his own convention of dialogue, his own prejudices and his own dislikes and jealousies of Pino's friends; and made Pino say things I know are not true. I shall have something more to say about this. It seems to me obvious that Pino did know English well and spoke it fluently, though with certain mistakes which gave it a peculiar flavour. And he was perfectly capable of writing those books himself, except that verbal correction would have been needed. This was too much trouble for Norman, who had very lofty ideas of himself as a writer, so he re-wrote Pino's books, and spoiled them, by taking out the special quality which was Pino and substituting his own much less amusing mannerisms. So, in reviving these memories I shall avoid looking at these two books until later on, trying to see Pino through my recollections, rather than through Norman's reconstruction of Pino's memories.

Pino told us, then, that he was born in the village of Alphonsine in Romagna. He had a curious double attitude towards Romagna, sometimes for and sometimes against. "All the highest job in Italy are in Romagnuoli hand," he assured me, but when I agreed that this was certainly true of Mussolini he went off on another tack, and explained his anti-Fascism on the grounds that he could not acknowledge a dictator who came from his own province: "Ozzerwise I would be for him!" And yet . . . On our way to Sicily we had to wait at Reggio di Calabria to get the car on the train ferry, and went into the station buffet. Pino moved off and we noticed that he was holding a most animated conversation with the bar-tender with whom he was drinking. Presently he came back to us radiant with pride: "He is a Romagnuolo! Have I not told you all the highest job in Italy are in Romagnuoli hand?" It would be a mistake to interpret that too literally as *naïveté*—there was certainly a side-shot intended at the Duce.

Another distinction of which Pino was abnormally proud was that he had been born or nearly born (I forget which) in a *manicomio*, a lunatic asylum. His mother, he would explain very gravely, had borne too many children in too short a time ("zhat bloody man," he would add in parenthesis, meaning his father) and consequently was weak in her head, and she had to be put '*là*' for a time. In his turbulent childhood this was a great asset to him, for often when he was about to be corrected they would suddenly recollect this disability or distinction—"*è nato là!*" they would say tapping their foreheads and Pino would escape his whipping.

Pino's father, an Aristophanic character, was the local sausage-maker. From many now forgotten stories of Pino's childhood I have an impression of him and his brothers and sisters huddled in a huge cavernous room with row upon row of *salami* hanging from the beams, the glow of red fires under enormous steaming pots, and a smell of cooked meat. According to Pino his father was one of the world's greatest sausage-makers and much appreciated by an intelligent public. Unfortunately he was an avowed anti-clerical and of a too convivial habit, weaknesses which led to his downfall. Pino taught Charles and me a song which he had from his father, beginning: '*Il molino* . . .' I've forgotten the rest. One of the stories about the sausage shop was that Pino's father one day picked up a dead donkey at a bargain price—since hearing some of Pino's stories I have rather gone off Italian sausages—and after a laborious day of turning it into every delicacy from brawn to *mortadella* sat down to promote a friendly glass. They had got about to the stage of singing '*Il molino*' when Pino's father unluckily remembered that he still had the donkey's head. Flown with rationalism and wine he and his friends nailed it—in some versions over the church, in others over the priest's house—and returned singing loudly. It was the beginning of his down-fall as a successful sausage-man.

After his father's failure Pino went to work in Florence, and the stories now took on a slightly improper tone which they seldom lost thereafter. His employer had an ugly wife—and as Pino acted her she was certainly hideous—who fell in love with Pino and tried to seduce this young Joseph from Romagna. (His name, by the way, was Giuseppe—hence Giuseppino—Pino—in Sicily Giu-seppuzzo, a saint of considerable influence owing to his position as *padre putativo di Nostro Signore*.) Our Giu-seppino strenuously rejected her advances, not, as he pointed out, from that strict virtue in which every young Roman Catholic is bred, but because he had an instinctive and unconquerable physical aversion from women. Astounded at this apparently unique indifference to her charms, this Florentine Madame Potiphar decided that Pino must have been bewitched into impotence by some evil-disposed person. She therefore took him to a *strega*, a witch or wise woman, who lived some distance out of

Florence, with a view to removing this disability by a counter-charm. It was at such moments that Pino's art shone as brightly as his eyes while he developed and at each performance improved the story. There was the long walk to the tumble-down cottage—Pino insisted on my driving there through impossibly stony narrow lanes, to prove the truth of the whole affair—the climbing of the stairs, the fearsome but comical appearance of the *strega*, who listened to the plaint of the lady and then made an unwelcome and too intimate examination and palping of Pino's person, leading to the muttered verdict: *"Normale! normale!"* I forget what the charms were—they used to vary—but I seem to remember a dried toad and a hair from Pino's head tied round an egg. Anyway they turned out to be quite useless, and Pino lost his job.

This squalid idyll usually led to the less interesting episode of Lavdomia, which must nevertheless have been important to Pino. Lavdomia was an unmarried Florentine girl, and Pino's father (hearing rumours perhaps of the *strega* adventure) decided that Pino was to marry her. "He would have marry me, zhat bloody man, to a *vumman!*" It is impossible to convey either the vehemence of Pino's utterance or the look of consternation on his face, an expressive *horror feminae* I should not have thought possible. For once it was no joke, and he was deadly serious—to marry Lavdomia would have been a sort of suicide to him. That *strega's* verdict can only have been partly true.

How Pino escaped the awful catastrophe of marriage with Lavdomia I can't remember—it may have been then that he realised his best opening would be in England. Pino liked to follow up some of his stories by a pilgrimage to the actual site, which he seemed to think was a guarantee that every fantastic detail he invented was true.

I have mentioned how he made me nearly wreck my car by going to see the *strega's* house. Well, we also had to go and see Lavdomia's house, a tall building near the Porta Romana. As we stood in the street, Pino went over it all again with his customary vehemence and gestures. Passers-by looked at us curiously, but nobody stopped. They may have thought Pino was an agent trying to sell me the house we were looking at.

A longer expedition, which pleased him very much, arose out of his assertion that outside Romagna the only place where you could find good *soprasata* (brawn) was in one of the small hill towns between Florence and Siena. Was it Montalcino or Montichiello? I forget, but I remember the brawn had cinnamon in it and was good, though not noticeably better than others. This was the sort of expedition Pino greatly approved. On the impulse of a chance remark to throw up whatever plans for business or pleasure one had made, and spend the morning or afternoon driving sixty or seventy miles over mountainous side roads to buy a few slices of brawn, which could have been bought, probably, just as well in Florence within a hundred yards—such a fantasy delighted him.

In much the same spirit he liked to stop the car when we were far out in the country and have a picnic meal at the house of some peasant-proprietor he knew. I remember once he found us a delicious picnic of new home-made bread, farm butter, anchovies washed in wine, and one of the best flasks of Chianti I ever tasted. At such moments Pino was at his best and happiest, without Norman's rather sneering cynicism to pull him down. Pino was a good cook, but very often the frugal peasant in him preferred such simple fare to the complex and out-of-the-way dishes Norman liked at that time.

These acted stories of Pino's had some of the quality of

the Scarpetta Neapolitan farces. And, of course, for his English friends there was the unexpectedness or personal pronunciation of his English. As I have said, he spoke English fluently, and in my experience very seldom had to hunt for a word; but some of our little habits of speech eluded him. In speaking, though not, curiously enough, in writing, he often failed to give the 's' of our plurals. Though he constantly heard us calling Prentice 'Charles' he always made it 'Charl'. Occasionally he came out with scraps of forgotten pre-1914 slang—'it give me the jim-jam' was a nice one. Like most Latins he was baffled by 'th' and made it a 'z' or an 's'. Most singular in one who knew English so well were Sam Weller transpositions of the letters 'v' and 'w', which look rather silly when written down but were very effective in speech.

Needless to say, as Pino was rightly proud of his English, we had to be extremely careful never to laugh *at* his mistakes, only *with* them, when he was trying to make us laugh, and did not know that his little mannerisms added to the fun. There was one occasion when I had to use such efforts not to laugh or even smile that I had a pain in the diaphragm for hours afterwards. I have entirely forgotten why, but I happened to mention one day the name of a Londoner who was evidently no friend of Pino's. He looked into my face with his large brown eyes troubled with resentment, and then said with emphatic gravity:

"Zhat man? He is a *vurm!*"

It was the unexpectedness which made it sound so funny, but of course if I had given any sign of amusement Pino would have insisted on knowing why, and as I am a very poor hand at deception he might have found out the real reason.

He was quite convinced that his interchange of 'v' and 'w' was the correct pronunciation, and that in spite of the fact that he heard English talked every day. The most striking example occurred when he and I (without Norman) were lunching at the Nuova Toscana. A youngish Florentine lawyer whom Pino knew came over to speak to him, was introduced, and talked to me in almost flawless English. When he had left I made the mistake of praising it, which of course instantly inflamed Pino's jealousy—he did not want us to have other Italian friends or to have any rival as a linguist. Pino undertook to put me right here, very persuasively, but firmly and confidently.

"Naw, my dear boy," he said, "you do not mean zhat. You do not know vot you are saying. Zhat man, he do not really know English. He make mistake. Now, when I say 'veal' I mean the 'veal' that go round; and when I say 'wheel' I mean the 'wheel' you eat. Zhat bloody man he do not know."

How much English Pino knew when he arrived friendless and nearly penniless in pre-1914 London it is impossible to say, but some time after his arrival he set out to instruct Londoners in Italian according to a 'pleasant method' he had worked out and so described in his advertisements. His memories of this epoch seemed to improve with age, and I distinctly remember his telling me that feeling he should dress in a dignified manner, both for his own sake and to do honour to so great a city, he bought himself a silk hat, long frock-coat, canary-coloured fancy waistcoat and very florid socks. I regret very much that I didn't see him. There were of course various adventures with pupils, one of whom was Crippen, the murderer of his wife. According to Pino, he was employed to give Italian lessons when the man was planning this horrid deed, and Pino inferred that Crippen had intended to fly to Italy after committing it. However, he changed his mind, discontinued the lessons, and was arrested when he landed in Montreal. It was always a sorrow to Pino that he had not more carefully cultivated this interesting person.

I have to confess that the coy look on Pino's face when he mentioned his 'pleasant method' rather aroused my suspicions that there might have been something a little *louche* about it. Apparently I did him a grave injustice, for going through Charles's letters I find one dated May 1932, when Pino was in London, which contains this paragraph:

"Poor Pino has a fegato and is compelled to live on Pellegrino. He seems cheerful, none the less, so I hope he is getting better. I had a most marvellous Prima Lezione ('Pleasant Method—vot I taught Crippen and ze Voolf') with drawings of the insides of an osteria, a restaurant and a hotel bedroom, all the objects with their Italian names. In the margin were dialogues in which I was interlocutor with a padrone, a waiter, &c., demanding triglie and so on."

It wouldn't surprise me if some of those dialogues verged on the improper.

The mention of Woolf is a reminder that Pino migrated to Cambridge and applied his 'pleasant method' of teaching Italian to various undergraduates. He claimed that he met Oscar Browning there, and had a Boccaccio tale (which I have forgotten) of how Oscar Browning came to see Pino in Florence accompanied by an extremely supercilious undergraduate who, Pino insisted, was named 'Greensleeves'. He must have known Lytton Strachey too. At any rate at the time of Lytton Strachey's death I had been praising his books and the very nice letter of appreciation he had sent Norman, and then tactlessly—I was always forgetting Pino was one of 'them'—went on to deplore

certain alleged tendencies. Pino took me up at once:
"Naw, my dear boy, he vos a ——, but he vos not a bloody
——." Subtle distinction! Norman himself was apt to
describe some of the men he disliked as "the wrong kind of
sod, my dear." It was my misfortune never to meet any of
the right ones, except Pino and himself.

From there Pino started up as a bookseller in London in
partnership with a young Jewish friend from Cambridge.
In making this partnership, so Pino assured me, he was
piously carrying out the pondered advice of his father
(zhat bloody man) who had impressed on him that if ever
he did take a partner, he must be a Jew, and then they
would be sure to make money. He also assured me that at
one year's end when their books did not show the profits
they had hoped for Pino upbraided his friend indignantly:
"Vot is the good of you being a Jew if you do not make
money for us?"

I knew Pino as far back as 1913-14, but without the
slightest suspicion of his real quality. The shop was far too
expensive for me, but I sometimes tried to pick up Italian
books from what was haughtily described as 'the rubbish'.
There was something very attractive about Pino even on
such slight acquaintance, and I met him again during the
1914-18 War when he was attached to the Italian Mission,
and he and his chief, Cippico, tried to get me transferred
to their 'pleasant method' of making war—in which of
course they failed. Pino had two versions of how he
managed to attain the improbable post of Italian King's
Messenger—one, which he gives in his book, through some
complicated wangling in Italy; the other, more picturesque,
through the pacifist politician, John Burns, who thought
Pino had such a nice smile he oughtn't to be killed.

Naturally this King's Messenger job produced its

blossoms of acted stories. He would begin by looking very serious and telling how he had been ordered to take a most important document from the British War Office to deliver to the Italian Commander-in-Chief in person. The despatch on specially thin paper was carried in a small box fitted on a belt under his tunic, and he was warned that if he was in any danger of being captured by the enemy he must instantly eat the despatch. Also, if he lost the despatch he would be shot. Well, at that point, any amateur of Piniana could see drama coming, and it was this. On the long train journey Pino made friends with some British officers, and finding they had several hours to wait at a junction they went off to a night-club to dance with girls. Finding his despatch belt a nuisance Pino took it off, and when they again reached the station discovered that he had lost it. Imagine how we suffered with him in his agonised expectation that the girls were probably spies and he would be shot at dawn, until at last the despatch was recovered just in time to catch the train! Like other great artists Pino could sometimes continue beyond the main climax without losing interest. When at last, after other sufferings I have forgotten, he reached Italian G.H.Q. the General put aside the despatch without looking at it, and remarked chattily: *"C'é la nebbia à Londra?"*— foggy in London?

On his next journey he had to take the same General a quantity of Nubian Boot Polish. When he asked if he was expected to eat it if captured, he was told sternly: *"Orioli, non fà lo spiritoso—Orioli,* do not be vitty."

There were several versions of another King's Messenger story. It seems that King George was sending a present of English porcelain (in war time?) to King Victor Emmanuel. The precious ware was packed in a large barrel which was then chained to Pino's person, with orders not to lose sight of it until he handed it over at the Quirinal. 'Zhat damn barrel of pot for Vittorio Emmanuele,'chained to its transporter, aroused coarse mockery from all the licentious Allied soldiery Pino encountered. He arrived in Paris during some crisis of the war when 'everyone have the jim-jam', and there were no porters, no taxis, nothing to eat, and Pino like an unwilling Diogenes had to roll his tub up and down the Gare du Nord looking for succour. Even when, in the last stages of exhaustion, he reached the royal palace in Rome he was met with the utmost suspicion and had great difficulty in finding an official who was ready to receive and sign for it. The end was Pino's sighed conviction that "*il Ré* never bothered to open zhat bloody barrel".

I don't know when Pino became friends with Douglas or when he returned to Florence as an antiquarian bookseller. Nor do I know where and how he picked up his knowledge of old books. His two great finds were a folio Shakespeare and a Tasso or Ariosto—I forget which—with notes in the author's handwriting. The former was sold in London for several hundred pounds, and the latter was bought by the Italian Government. I once saw him pick up a book from a barrow on the Lungarno after joking with the man. It looked like a rubbishy schoolbook to me, but Pino afterwards claimed there were collectors of such things and that he made a hundred lire by it. On the other hand, as the slump of the 'thirties persisted, his bookselling business, he used to complain, practically ceased.

Life was not easy for Pino under the Fascist *régime*, in spite of his being from Romagna. He was under suspicion because he was always with English friends, and was hauled up and questioned. He got out of that by showing that he still had a partner in England, and that his book

D

sales were nearly all to England and America. Then one night he got drunk in a restaurant and was rude to four blackshirts, who seized the poor little man as he came out, threw him on the ground and stamped on his face, grinding the broken glass of his spectacles into his face and, as they hoped, his eyes with their hobnailed boots. By a miracle his eyes were saved, and he managed to find his way to Norman's flat. They knew a doctor who was no friend of the *régime* and he dressed Pino's face, so that he could take the next train to Venice, where he stayed until his wounds healed and he could return to Florence.

In December, 1930, when Norman had his sixty-second birthday, Pino was forty-six, not far short of forty-seven. At that period of life that difference of fifteen years— always considerable—was of great importance. At sixty-two Douglas had lost much of his fire and energy; what had been 'consuming passion' dragged on without dignity as rather squalid vice; he had lost all his old interests, writing had become a bore—he wanted to take things easy, to be amused and stimulated. And there was Pino with his boundless vitality and gift of entertainment, his stories and his memories of peasant life, always at hand. It was a great thing for a small-scale antiquarian bookseller, son of a sausage-maker, to be taken up as the most intimate friend of Norman Douglas. Pino was very proud of it, nearly as proud as he was (in 1930) of his friendship with Lawrence, which Norman gradually nagged and edited into a wholly improbable hostility. But though Pino was so much the younger man he had not Douglas's great strength of constitution. He took no exercise, except when Norman made him. He smoked too many cigarettes, ate and drank too much, which resulted in a '*fegato*'—a liver—and a dreary *régime* of mineral water which always collapsed too soon into festivity. I shall have more to say

about this later on, but that future biographer must pay
great attention to Pino when he comes to this section of
Douglas's life. The danger for him will be that Pino will
steal the show. He was not only a much more lovable
person than Douglas, but—at any rate to non-Italians—a
more amusing and attractive character. Both Norman and
Pino were jealous and malicious, but while in Pino's case
the manifestations were so obvious as to be forgivable—as
in a naughty child—with Douglas they ran deep and
rancorous. But in those Florentine days Pino was truly
what Reggie Turner hoped to be—the life and soul of the
party.

3

IT is some indication of the affection the Lawrences had for Pino that Frieda Lawrence, feeling rather lonely, thought she would spend the first Christmas after her husband's death with Pino. *Enfant terrible* that he was, he showed me a Teutonically sentimental letter she had written him (in English) to say she was coming. The chance which had brought me to Florence at the same time involved me all unawares in another situation.

Lawrence's will had been lost, and for a time his estate had to be administered as that of an intestate, with the result of a confused situation with Lawrence's family on the one side and Frieda on the other. After she had given up so much for him and stood by him in his troubles, it was wrong that she should not have her reward, at least in money, now that he was dead and famous and within a few years of being taken up by the parasitical professors and 'critics' who had done nothing for him in his lifetime. There were other problems. In recognition of his part in distributing *Lady Chatterley's Lover*, Frieda wanted Pino to issue small limited editions of Lawrence's posthumous books in his Lungarno Series. But there was the question of what publisher should produce the library edition, and of course Pino could not undertake so large a book as the *Letters*. Finally there was the problem of what to do if, as seemed certain, all Lawrence's earlier English copyrights came on the market.

We had some anxious discussion about all this, and I soon realised that neither Frieda nor Pino knew anything much about publishing or about business methods and, if I may say so, business ethics. I didn't realise it at the time, but it was very fortunate for Frieda that Douglas wasn't there, for he was not only full of malice, even against Lawrence dead, but he had the *idée fixe* of the amateur writer that the publisher is out to rook authors, whereas the plain fact is that publishers have had to develop a special arsenal of defence to avoid being rooked daily by authors. I realised that something had to be done quickly and that we needed a clearer head than any of those present.

I remembered that my friend, A. S. Frere, then Managing Director of Heinemann, was spending Christmas in Cannes with Lady Russell and her friends, and eventually got a phone call through to him. I shall never forget the anguish of that call. The line was so infamously bad (and the charge extortionate compared with America, where you hear as plainly at 3,000 miles as at 300 yards) that I could make out nothing but what sounded like an English voice say unintelligible things. More accustomed to the wretched gadget than I was, Frere seemingly could hear what I said or some of it, and just after Christmas arrived in Florence.

I have sometimes wondered whether in my anxiety to help Frieda and give Frere the kudos of getting back all Lawrence's work to Heinemann (who first published him) I didn't unwittingly sell him a considerable stud of white elephants. There can't have been much profit out of *Phoenix* and *Apocalypse*, for example.

After much discussion, Frere agreed that he would issue the *Letters* and other posthumous works (allowing Pino his priorities and paying Frieda well for them), and also if possible take over all the other books and keep them in print—all of which he carried out loyally. The travesty of these events in Douglas's re-write of Pino's memoirs must be read to be believed. This is what he says:

"It was suggested that she (i.e. Frieda) should bring out a collection of Lawrence's letters, and I offered to accompany her to London to arrange for the publication of them. This was ultimately accomplished and I hope she made something of them, although I do not care for the tone of the letters themselves."

I have myself heard Pino rave about Lawrence's letters and boast proudly of his intimacy with the great man. The implication that Pino 'placed' the *Letters* with Heinemann's is a piece of cheek. The suppression of my small share in these transactions is characteristic of Douglas's editing and re-writing of Pino's memoirs.

On Christmas Eve, while we were waiting for Frere, Pino involved us in one of his adventures. He decided that the four of us—Frieda, B., and he and I—would have dinner and then go to hear midnight mass at the Church of the Annunziata. I have forgotten why that was the right place to go in Florence, but it undoubtedly was, for we could scarcely get even to the entrance. Sitting over dinner until after eleven had resulted in Pino's drinking a good deal of Chianti, and the cold air of a frosty night did the rest. Just inside the porch of the church was a sacred Presepio, and as the people streamed in they threw on it offerings in money which a cynical priest grinningly raked in with a croupier's sweep. This for some reason roused Pino's anti-clerical bile. "Look at him!" he said in a tremendously loud whisper. "Vot a ——! Naw, ve cannot stay here." So out we went into the freezingly cold

Piazza Annunziata, where there is a fine bronze equestrian statue of one of the Grand Dukes—Ferdinand I, I think. Anyway, on the large stone pedestal is a flat bronze shield embossed with bees. Pino assured us that nobody could ever count the number of these bees correctly, and pointed out that somebody or bodies had already been trying to tick them off with chalk and had desisted. Pino, however, was determined to count them that night.

It was very cold waiting, but fortunately he gave up after about ten minutes, during which the frost seemed to make him drunker, remarking: "Idn't it *funny* I cannot count zhose bloody bee?" We next entered an open and lighted church not far from the Duomo where a sermon in a strong Florentine accent was in progress. I couldn't catch much of it, but Pino soon announced in a too loud whisper: "Zhis bloody priest is a cretin—ve go in Duomo." So off we went to the great cathedral, which was in total darkness except for a light on the altar. The place was so dark after the lighted streets that we had felt our way some distance in before I suddenly realised that the whole huge building was full of silent people, waiting for mass, and all looking amazedly at our noisy progress. A verger came up in hostile mood, but Pino rose to the situation. Speaking perfect Florentine he said he and his friends had a devotion to Madonna, and wished to put up the largest and most expensive candle obtainable to the Madonna in a chapel of the south transept. This costly devotion mollified the verger, who led us to the holy statue. Pino purchased the most expensive candle there was, and advanced to light and place it at the shrine. Unfortunately, there was a wooden floor in the chapel (perhaps to protect some precious pavement) raised a few inches above the level of the transept. Pino failed to see it, tripped, and fell with a crash which re-echoed through the silent sonorouslyechoing cathedral. Then Frieda made a discovery. "He's drunk," she whispered to us.

I find from Charles's letters at the time that their humble writer friend seems to have been the cause of the two publishers meeting. At all events, under date 19th January, 1931, Charles writes me:

"I spent a heavenly evening with Frere on Thursday. He is a champion; one of the most delightful men I ever met. We were at Victoria when Pino and Frieda arrived on Friday evening, and on Saturday night Pino dined with me. He was superb. We went out to the flat afterwards, and talked till 5.30 a.m.—such stories, and ever so much about you and B. and N.D. Pino slept on two chairs, and disappeared after breakfast next morning."

It appears, too, that there were plans for trying to please Norman, and that the fearful toils of publishers sometimes admit of slight alleviations. I should perhaps first mention that at my suggestion Chatto's had started a series of short books at a low price which they called Dolphins. On 6th January, 1931, Charles wrote me:

"Your idea of getting Tomlinson to write a Dolphin about Douglas is great, and Frere is being perfect over it; he is going to approach Tomlinson himself, and he will inform Heinemann what is being done, so they will not feel aggrieved. An excellent notion. Douglas, as you doubtless know, is dedicating to Tomlinson the second edition of *London Street Games*. You will almost certainly know too that we are publishing it as a Dolphin. The series, of course, is mainly for new stuff, but Douglas is a law to himself, and the little book, though I doubt whether it will sell very many copies, is so curious and charming a piece of work that dolphinisation seemed the best course. I hope you will think so too."

You will observe the grasping cupidity of these publishers. Tomlinson was 'a Heinemann author'. As for Douglas telling me about his street boys book going into the Dolphins—he never mentioned it to me. Another reference to the Tomlinson book comes up in a letter from Charles of 23rd January, 1931. He says:

"Frere spoke to Tomlinson yesterday afternoon, who at first was unforthcoming, but gradually warmed up, and at the end was very enthusiastic. I have written off to him at once and made him an offer. I do hope he does the book, as I can well believe it would so stimulate N.D. Frere has been most magnanimous. I go to the circus with him, Pino, and Frieda tomorrow night. I am hugely delighted that he has got his way with these posthumous D.H.L.s."

I wonder if Douglas ever knew what Frere did to arrange that Tomlinson book on him of which Douglas was so proud? In view of the Orioli-Douglas account of the disposal of the Lawrence copyrights, I am tempted to make one more quotation from Charles's letters which otherwise I should have kept to myself:

"I am awfully glad that the Lawrence business has been settled up so successfully; Frieda certainly owes you a lot, for without your help Frere would not have been able to put the thing through." (Letter of 31st January, 1931.)

While Pino so chivalrously accompanied Frieda to
London, thinking, of course, entirely of her interests and
Lawrence's fame, and not in the least of the Lungarno
Series, I had the undeserved compensation of Norman's
company in Florence. No doubt he was rather lonely
without Pino, and was glad to have someone to talk to
over lunch or dinner. It did not seem to me that Norman's
talk was particularly witty—I can remember no clever
repartee or sparkling phrase which one had to pass on.
But others, who knew him earlier, have praised his wit, so
I can only conclude I was unlucky, or perhaps lucky, for I
have no liking for the professional wit or the noted
conversationalist. My general impression of his talk was of
its good sense, its contempt for shams and sentimentalities
("Cinquecento" as he called them), and range of knowledge
of a rather obsolescent kind. He seemed to me not to
want to monopolise the talk, as Pino too often did. What
Lawrence called his "wicked whimsicality" was not very
obvious either, though I suspect he enjoyed giving an
appearance of devil-may-care cynicism and disillusion—in
his youth people had still been Byronic. But he most
certainly had a gift for caricature in speech, with
humorous exaggerations which you might call whimsical.
To me the caricature was rather German than English or
Scotch or American, and used to remind me vaguely of the
drawings in the pre-1914 *Simplicissimus*. Underneath all
this I believe there was a good deal more warmth of
feeling than he cared to show. For instance, in the early
days of our acquaintance he never mentioned his sons,
except off-handedly as 'rascals' or 'ruffians', and so
forth, but when he found we didn't believe him and were
really interested in them he spoke of them with a good
deal of pride. Later on I got to know Archie Douglas,
and in the few surviving letters I have from Norman

I notice he several times speaks of Archie.

The capricious chance which has destroyed so many letters from Norman and Pino has preserved a curious little memorial of a lunch with Norman. On the back of a letter from Charles (dated 21st January, 1931) I find written in Norman's handwriting:

"Zwei Knaben standen vor der Thür,
    Die froren an die Beine;
    Der Andere fror nach Réaumur,
    Nach Celsius der Eine."

How did that scrap of German nonsense verse come into the talk? I have no idea. The interest of the thing is that Norman quotes it on page 344 of *Looking Back*, which he was perhaps then writing. If so he moved but slowly at first, for he notes somewhere that on 3rd January, 1932 (nearly a year later), he had reached page 431. He must have reached page 510 and the end early in February, for I find this in a letter from Charles of 11th February, 1932:

"I am greatly excited to hear that Norman has really finished his book. I was chary of worrying him with questions myself, but now I'll send him a line. I do wish he didn't bar cars; I'd gladly travel on the roof or the running board, if only he could be with us as well. What a delight it will be to have Pino. I am devoted to him, and count the hours until I see you all."

The last part of the letter refers to a projected motor tour through Southern Italy and Sicily, of which more later; but the book referred to was unquestionably *Looking Back*. Knowing how eager Charles was to read and publish that book I sent him word directly Norman told us it was done. Norman at that time was talking so cynically of publishers and frankly of needing money that I was afraid he might sell it to someone else if Charles didn't get in at once. I needn't have worried. Norman had the situation completely in control. He was perfectly well aware how greatly Charles admired him, and wanted to publish him, so that there was an excellent chance of getting more for the book than it was really worth from the purely economic point of view. This was just after the first depreciation of the paper pound, and Norman offered to sell the book outright for a thousand gold pounds. It needed a canny Scot to think of that. By an outright sale he could in those days escape the iniquitous tax on authors living abroad (full rate of income tax on every pound paid as royalties or advance on royalties), a kindly attention which authors owe to the American Congress and Sir Winston Churchill. Make a note of it. At the same time the stipulation for gold pounds protected him against further depreciation, though in fact he could not be paid in gold, only in paper calculated to equal gold. The good round sum was a stiff one for an author with a limited if faithful public, yet it was not so high as to be impossibly extortionate.

But Charles also was Scotch, and conscious of his obligations to his partners. He would have hated to involve them in a serious loss, and yet he was pining to add *Looking Back* to his long list of successes of esteem. Evidently much pondering went on, for our Sicilian trip had come and gone, and the year had reached the end of May and still there was no decision. On 30th May, 1932, I find Charles writing me, very cautiously:

"Norman writes very kindly about his book, giving us heaps of time to chew it over, but I don't know yet what will be the decision."

When they did at last decide to take the book Charles's pleasure at getting it was decidedly tempered by Greenock caution:

"We are doing Norman's book, and all is settled save the signing of the documents. It has been a big pull, and we shall not be able to do the same thing for a good long time; very likely we may have been silly, but Norman's case is exceptional, and it would be difficult to think of another that was." (1st July, 1932.)

I hope I was unfair, but I took the latter part of that paragraph (with a chuckle) as a warning that I wasn't to imagine that I could start putting forward any such claims. In the whole of Charles's correspondence I think that is the only sign of what you might call publisher's caution toward me, and with the aching hollow after the extraction of that thousand-pounds gold tooth I can well understand it. Later on in the same letter Charles cheered up and tried to look on the bright side:

"I am very happy that the 'Yesterday' business—for that's the title—has been fixed up."

The title of course was eventually changed to the better one of *Looking Back*, but here surely is an example of handsome treatment by a publisher, while if anyone was 'swindled' in the transaction it certainly wasn't the author. Chatto's attempt to solve the problem of getting home on this book was clever. They had certain facts to go on. Norman and Pino together had issued one hundred copies of *Capri Materials* at three guineas, and had sold them. Norman complains that the book was so costly they had only thirty pounds to share between them. He omits to say that, using the same print and blocks, Pino in 1930, printed off another 525 copies at thirty shillings. In January, 1931, Pino gave me number 466, and if he was selling them in numerical order he then had only thirty-four copies remaining, for numbers 500-525 were for gift and review. Chatto's published almost the same number— 535—of *Looking Back* in two handsome volumes, very much nicer than any Lungarno Series production, at three guineas, if I remember right. If those went off quickly, a substantial part of the advance would have been recovered, but it must have been difficult to sell a library edition of such a large book cheaply. It is not my intention to pry into trade secrets, merely to show that on this occasion Norman put over a fast one on his friend. Will it be credited that the only acknowledgment of this generous treatment in Norman's *Late Harvest* is a grumble that Chatto's did not use all the illustrations he sent in! The small (!) additional expense, he thought, would have been made up by the interest of the photographs. He proposed to omit two photographs of himself and to add nine, including The Weaste, Manchester; Professor Leydig; and a striped salamander. I may remind the reader that in July, 1932, the world slump was close to that startling moment when President Hoover left the White House slamming behind him the doors of all the banks in the U.S.A. The addition of seven expensive blocks, of such palpitating interest, to such a book would surely have been a wise investment on the part of the publisher.

It is as hard for a man of literary occupation to write sensibly and justly about himself as it is for him to write about his own books. The unavoidable dwelling on self has to be done with skill to avoid, at any rate, the appearance of vanity and egotism—and too much self-depreciation is as bad as too much self-glorification. In *Looking Back*, which is essentially autobiographical, Douglas found an ingenious solution of the difficulty. Instead of the usual from cradle to one foot in the grave narrative, he hit upon the device of picking out one by one the names of friends recorded on the visiting cards he had gradually collected, during a life-time, and had preserved in a large bronze bowl. This in itself was characteristic. Norman was a born collector, a Jonathan Oldbuck of the nineties, for who but a maniacal collector would keep such rubbish through a life of financial cataclysms and flights? The loss of his valuable collection of rare pamphlets on Capri may have discouraged his continuing whatever book on the subject he had in mind, though there was the additional objection that the topic was so hackneyed that nothing much remained to be discovered or said. A history of Brighton would be a more promising theme. But having kept these cards, he at last found this use for them—if indeed he did actually use them and not merely imagine them. The plan certainly had advantages. By seeming to write always of people he had known he was able to write at length about himself and yet avoid the appearance of egotism and vanity which is such a snare in autobiography. He was sixty and tired, above all tired of writing, which had never been a real passion with him. The difficult art of construction was not his—all his books, even the best, are essay-length pieces skilfully linked together—though an autobiography is almost self-constructing. But the proportion of the parts needs as much care as finding the right tone. His visiting cards gave him a series of pegs, on each of which he could hang just as much as he cared to say and no more, while the device enabled him to take an informal tone and so avoid the ridiculous pomposity inseparable from a Proustian *A la Recherche de Moi-même*, of which we have had several volumes too many. As a

purely personal preference I put *Looking Back* immediately
after the excellent three—*South Wind*, *Old Calabria* and
Siren Land—and above Norman's other books.

But, as Norman himself points out, there were obvious
drawbacks. One is that this haphazard picking out of
names had the unforeseen disadvantage of concentrating
too much attention on some periods of his life and leaving
others almost unnoticed. He does not point out that it
also resulted in a certain amount of padding, perhaps not
altogether unwelcome to an author scant o' breath. How
can any reader feel interested in finding on the aggregate
some dozens of names unknown to him with no more
meaty comment than '?' or 'a blank' or 'he has slipped my
memory' or 'I remember nothing about him'? If so, why
mention him at all? An autobiography is not a cemetery,
though Norman had a passion for visiting cemeteries and
reading the meaningless lines of names unknown to him.
And I have sometimes wondered if all the cards were
genuine. When, I wonder, did Mr. D. H. Lawrence buy
himself visiting cards and leave one on Mr. Norman
Douglas? But the card may date from Lawrence's school-
master days and have been sent in to the Assistant Editor of
The English Review.

I think a case might be made out for the view that *Looking
Back* is not really so casual and haphazard as it looks.
Without making a close scrutiny—which is a job for that
biographer—I think I can show that he says something
about almost every year from 1876 to 1928, the earlier
years being practically blank and the 1920s scantily
represented, no doubt because the use of visiting cards
declined, as Norman himself says. I used to have difficulty
in remembering whether he was born in 1868 or 1869 (it
was 1868) but I never forget the day of the year on account
of a little characteristic episode—he always liked to get

even the smallest fact right, and in 1931 he was beginning
to worry about a memory which was still better than most
people's. Walking back from Bianca's one winter night
Norman remarked that his birthday was on the most
ridiculously inappropriate of Catholic festivals—"And
damn it, I can't remember which one." We suggested
everything we could think of from the Nativity to the
Ascension, but no, none of them was right. He was still
openly worrying about it when we parted outside the
Gran Bretagna. Suddenly, as we waited for the lift, the
outer revolving door of the hotel turned violently,
Norman's tall form emerged and called: "I have remembered! It was the Immaculate Conception!" and rushed
out again. Got that fact! Make a note of it!

He was therefore born on December 8th, but where?
In Scotland or in Vorarlberg? Or was it at Falken-
horst, Thuringia?* I assume rather from vague memories
of what he said than from any text that he spent most of
his early years in Vorarlberg, at least until the time when
his father was killed by falling off a mountain. This
obviously was a disaster for the family, and had especially
unfortunate results for Norman. This handsome, spirited,
wilful, brilliant boy and young man needed above all things
the influence and authority of an intelligent and strong-
willed father, which apparently he was. The loss of that
guidance just when it was most needed was the reason for
most of his errors and follies. The women who brought
Norman up were evidently quite unable to cope with him.
And you have only to look at the photograph of the
handsome, reckless lad to see why it was that he turned
into the 'well-bred cad', to use his phraseology, of 1892.

The following rough schedule, taken without over-

* I owe this information to Mr. Martin Secker. But Mr. Fitz Gibbon
says Vorarlberg.

E

much attention to precise detail, should give a first outline
of the mere facts of Douglas's life even to those who know
little or nothing of his books. That biographer of course
will correct, supplement and greatly expand all this. I
assume Douglas was mainly in Vorarlberg from 1869 to
1878. Thereafter:

1876 Visited London and Deeside.

1877 Visited London again.

1878 Sent to England. School at Yarlet Hall, Stafford-
shire

1878–80 School changed at his whim to Mowsley
Rectory, Leicestershire.

1881 To Uppingham School. Disliked it, and persuaded
his mother to move him to the Gymnasium at
Karlsruhe, where there was no surveillance, and
the schoolboys kept mistresses. This move was
made in October 1882.

1883–1889 Karlsruhe. His vacations must have been
spent either in Vorarlberg or Scotland.

1886 He mentions being in Bregenz (Vorarlberg) on the
3rd September.

1888 His first visit to Italy. He went to Capri for the
famous blue lizards on the Faraglione rocks, and
fell in love with the Bay of Naples.

1889 Left Karlsruhe school in July. Was in London on
the 7th October. Cycling in southern France
14th–26th October. Paris in November.

1890 Returned to neighbourhood of Karlsruhe to
geologise. To London. In June at East Sheen.
Visited Oxford.

1891 London. Re-visited Uppingham, and still loathed
it. To the Shetland Islands. Clifton (near Bristol).
March-April, the island of Vulcano. May, took

rooms in Walsingham House, Piccadilly, a
haunt of the *jeunesse dorée* of that time.

1892 London, and in April–May a tour of Malta,
Brindisi, Corfu, Patras, Athens, Sorrento, Amalfi,
Cava.

1893 London. Passed the necessary exams and entered
the Foreign Office.

1894 Attached to H.B.M.'s Embassy, St. Petersburg.
Made a tour of Finland.

1895 St Petersburg. Visited Warsaw, Constantinople,
Smyrna, and Anatolia. Affairs with Russian
women.

1896 St. Petersburg. Visited Moscow. In November
fled precipitately from Russia to avoid serious
consequences following the discovery of his love
affair with 'Helen', hinted at by him as being of
very high rank. Says he went voluntarily *en
disponibilité*. Bought a villa near Posilipo, but
spent his Christmas in Paris.

1897 Posilipo. Yachting cruise with the American
author, Marion Crawford, to Elba and Corsica.
Also visited that year Capri, Meran and Vorarlberg,
Paris and London. His marriage must have been
about this time.

1898 India in January–February. Posilipo. Divonne,
Switzerland. Back to Posilipo, where a son born in
December.

1899 Posilipo. Summer in Vorarlberg.

1900 Visited Tunisia and Ceylon.

1901 London.

1902 Mentions being in Sorrento.

1903 Naples, Capri.

1904 Mentions being in Capri on 18th October.

1905 Mentions being in Naples on the 1st May.

1906 A blank.

1907 In Capri early spring. I infer that much of the period 1900–1906 was spent on Capri, but perhaps not.

1908 Visited Æolian islands. Was on Ischia in April. Began to write *Siren Land*.

1909 In the January issue of *Putnam's and the Reader* appeared his article on E. A. Poe, which he considered his 'first appearance before the literary world' as distinct from his antiquarian and scientific papers. (He was then 40.) In June he was in South Italy, visited Messina to bring help to the victims of the earthquake. London. In December, back to Tunisia to write a commissioned book, *Fountains in the Sand*.

1910 January-March, Tunisia. London.

1911 London. Tour of Calabria. Called on Joseph Conrad at Ashford, Kent. In September, at Yarmouth.

1912 London. In December his first mention of *English Review*, though it had published his *Typhoeus* in February, 1909 and the first chapter of *Siren Land* in May 1909.

1913 Assistant Editor of *English Review*. 27th May, mentions being at Positano. Back to London.

1914 In April visited Charles Doughty at Eastbourne.

1915 Summer in Suffolk. *English Review* mentioned, December.

1916 A blank. Sometime in 1916 he received through Humbert Wolfe an intimation that he had to leave England, though nothing is said of this in *Looking Back*.

1917 Italy. At Modane on his way to France on 13th October. Montmartre. *South Wind* published.

1918 Paris. Spring and summer at St Malo. Paris until

12th December. Mentone, 15th December. That autumn and winter in state of destitution.

1919   Menton. In April tour through Provence with Mr. R.—Arles, Nîmes, Avignon, Sorgues, Vaucluse, Orange. In Florence in November at latest.

1920   Florence. Greece for 'longish period'. Skyros.

1921–4   Blank, but Florence and Italian excursions.

1925   Kenya and Florence.

1926   Florence and Capri on 26th August.

1927   Blank.

1928   Florence and in spring to Baalbek.

1929–1952   Not accounted for in *Looking Back*.

I have added one or two facts from other sources, otherwise the whole of that chronology may be found in *Looking Back*. It does give a fragmentary outline or synopsis of his life; and the autobiography is not the aimless collection of scraps some people think, but does have a certain time-and-place structure. The defect of the visiting-cards device must be obvious to every reader of the book, for it is almost wholly concentrated on two epochs of his life which taken together make up only sixteen years—the schooldays at Karlsruhe (1883-1889) and the ten years (1897-1908) in Southern Italy. Other epochs are mentioned of course, but incidentally, and there are many omissions.

Possibly from 'gentlemanly' scruples, Douglas makes no mention of his wife in this book, and of course I never questioned him on the subject. It was only recently and by chance that I even learned her name. Yet he did sometimes speak of her, never in any derogatory way that I remember although I am bound to admit that his utterances about her usually started with the formula, "Give the devil her due . . . !" and ended up with his sardonic

"Ha!" He did mention that his being a Scot and able to prove the *animus revertendi* (i.e. intention of returning to take up domicile) got him out of an awkward scrape during his divorce proceedings, the Scottish law being apparently less idiotic than the English. I remember his saying that Mrs. Douglas went with him on his first tour of Tunisia (1900) and that ('give the devil her due') she had been very plucky about climbing mountains under conditions of real hardship. Pino had a story that, when they were on the point of separating, Norman for days on end refused to make any answer to her but 'Mew'! It sounds very like him. The remainder of Norman's confidences on this subject are hardly publishable, and I should not reveal them even if they were.

The material of *Looking Back* must have been very much in his consciousness during 1931-2, for I heard a good many of the tales from him before I read them in the book. One of the most interesting, the story of the 'Helen' on whose account he left Russia and the Foreign Office so hurriedly, is left unfinished in *Looking Back*. According to what he told me she was of so high a rank that any open scandal would have been death to them both. Norman got over the frontier just ahead of the Russian secret police, and when his train reached Berlin he was handed a long telegram from Petersburg in a language wholly unknown to him and the friends he consulted. It was, he assumed, a message from 'Helen', perhaps some plan for them to meet somewhere, but as he could not read the message he was helpless. Thirty years later he discovered (I forgot to ask how) that it was Siamese transliterated. The temptation to have it read was very strong, but he resisted, because to have found out what she had said might have brought one more endless regret. If this decision shows his usual self-protection, it is also the sole occasion in my acquaintance with him when he showed any real sentiment about a woman.

I liked, and still like, that story better than any of the others he told me, but have long been haunted by Dr. Johnson's cynical though irrefutable remark that "seldom any splendid story is wholly true," and have wondered if this tale of the lovely Russian aristocrat is 'wholly true'. Personally I believe it entirely. Of course, in the warfare of daily life Norman would not have had the slightest hesitation in perjuring himself a dozen times daily if he judged it expedient. And, of course, both in talk and writing he indulged that gift of his for amusing caricature to the point where the exaggeration becomes preposterous—think, for example, of that fantastic pursuit of the chicken in *Rain on the Hills*. But when he told the story he was quite serious. Admittedly he had more vanity than pride, but so far as my experience goes he lacked that silly vanity which can never resist playing for false *réclame* and admiration by boasting—improving or inventing 'good stories' to the greater glory of the teller. I have since detected him in alterations of the truth both in his re-writings of Pino's books and in *Late Harvest*, but I think the 'Helen' story was true. Moreover, when he was not animated by fantasy or malice, he was (I believe) rather scrupulously accurate in his reminiscences if only because his scientific and antiquarian pursuits had made precision a habit. Note how careful he is, when citing a book, nearly always to give the exact edition and page, and how even in *Late Harvest* he takes the trouble to correct little blunders and pen-slips in earlier books. The curious story about the death of Ludwig of Bavaria (*Looking Back*, p. 9) shows him correcting a vivid memory when his diary proved that what he remembered could not have happened.

To me it is always a pleasure to re-read *Looking Back* if

only for the sake of the writing, which has such clean phrasing, such unpedantically right structure of language. I find in it no tricks, affectations, pretentiousness, striving for effect, running after witticisms, self-consciousness or abstractions trying to appear profound. It is written in the style of a man who is master of his thought and of how to express his meaning. There was no pose of fine writing about Douglas as there was, for instance, about Conrad and his imitators. I don't think I ever heard Norman talk about 'prose' or 'style', except perhaps by inference from some literary judgment. Yet, at any rate in *Looking Back* (and I think in other books), he achieves the difficult success of saying exactly what he wishes to say, neither more nor less, economically, vigorously and lucidly. What he lacked, as his novels show, was not style but invention. His prose had that natural dignity which he retained in spite of his scallywag behaviour, and also that decent *propreté* which always distinguished his linen and comely white hair. It is quite truly a classical prose, as far from the finicky elegance of Walter Pater's writing as from banal neatness, that peculiar instinct for regularised ugliness so characteristic of English life.

Well, if a man has not learned to write well by the time he is sixty there is not much hope for him. Yet Norman went through a long period of search and apprenticeship before he learned to write such good English. Perhaps the German education may have been a handicap. Ford Madox Hueffer, who was also half German, half English, used to say that German was a danger to an English writer, and would point to the dreadful examples of Carlyle and Queen Victoria—though there is a great deal to be said for the Queen's writing. In Norman's case the difficulties of being an Anglo-German may have been complicated by service in the Foreign Office. The peculiar jargon of

PHOTOGRAPH OF NORMAN DOUGLAS'S BUST

(From the photograph in the possession of Mr. William Dibben)

Io col gatto inviamo auguri.

PINO ORIOLI AND HIS CAT

NORMAN DOUGLAS AND ORIOLI ON A WALKING TOUR
IN THE VORARLBERG

CHARLES PRENTICE

Costume di gala Albanese

PICTURE POST-CARD OF WOMAN IN CALABRIAN COSTUME
BOUGHT AT THE SAME TIME AS POST-CARD IN ORIOLI'S
BOOK

24.3.32

Dearest Richard,

Your cable from Bagnara was waiting for me, & this evening there is a whole flight of cards from Reggio & Bagnara. I wish I could retaliate properly, but I got off ones at Rome & Paris. Since then — what? Bandhuia was a travelling paradise, but where are you all now? I have been utterly lost since I wrote to consciousness on Monday turning somewhere about Naples.

FACSIMILE OF PART OF A LETTER FROM CHARLES PRENTICE

(See page 91)

7th March 1934

My dearest Richard,

I have been to Monticatini with my brother-in-law for the
week end and only yesterday I found your letter with
the contents. You are too generous and too good to me,"
and I have no words for thanking you, I only wished
you had been here when I open the letter and I should
have jumped to your neck and kissed you. I shall
never, never forget you, spontaneous act of generosity
and you will have my gratitude for ever and ever.

FACSIMILE OF PART OF A LETTER FROM ORIOLI

(See pages 167–168)

Le Glacier

BRASSERIE - BAR - CAFÉ
ANTIBES (A.-M.)
PLACE MACÉ
TÉLÉPH. 401·02

R. C. Antibes. 4.820

ANTIBES, le _____

1 Place Macé
Antibes A.M.
24 July 1939

My dear Richard
I have just run into
Frere — or rather, he has run into
me — and that reminds me that
I never thanked you for writing
the admirable article (far too
flattering, of course, but why not?)
about me. But I am sorry to
hear from Frere that you think of
staying in America. What is this?
Please drop me a line, and say
when you are coming back to
Europe. I haven't seen you since
Canadel, and want to see you again.
Heaps of love to Netta   always
Norman

FACSIMILE OF A LETTER FROM NORMAN DOUGLAS

(See pages 173–174

government documents cannot be much help to any young man's prose, and members of the Foreign Office worsen the situation by a fatal delusion that they are born witty.

As a matter of fact Douglas's first traceable publication was in German, *Zur Fauna Santorins*, 1892. The very subject of the essay shows accomplishments rarely possessed by a handsome young Scotsman about town who, as he was fond of repeating, spent most of his youth and early manhood 'consumed with passion' for a seemingly endless series of young women. It was, to say the least, unusual for such a person to write an article in German for a scientific periodical. It was, perhaps, less unusual for a young buck to have visited Santorin, a volcanic island in the Sporades, but it would not be customary for the average Piccadilly swell to have any scientific knowledge of lizards, sea-gulls and fleas, which, I assume, make up the bulk of the island's fauna.

I don't think Douglas says anywhere why he wrote that essay in German—it will be a point for that biographer to investigate. At all events, his published writings after that were all in English. In 1894 he enriched the world with essays on *The Beaver in Norway*, *The Herpetology of Baden* and *The Avifauna of Baden*. These were followed in 1895 by *Pumice Stone Industry* and in 1896 by *On the Darwinian Hypothesis*. The only one of these I have read is *The Herpetology of Baden*, reprinted in *Three of Them*, and I am bound to confess the experience made me think of a favourite exclamation of the author—'Uphill work!' And so calamitously unretentive is my memory that I could not name a single lizard native to the former Grand Duchy. Yet it strikes me that frogs, snakes and lizards are far better topics for a young writer than the usual hackneyed literary figures from Mallarmé to Kierkegaarde or the

sterner gamut from Marx to Marx. Lizards are lively.
They must first be caught and, if possible, without loss of
tail. When caught, if they are to be written about, they
must be precisely described and identified, and the
literature hunted up in some scientific library. Problems
of various kinds come up to exercise the intelligence.
Why, for instance, is there a special breed or sub-species
of blue lizard on the Faraglione rocks and not on Capri
itself? I don't think that question has ever been satis-
factorily answered, and that, of course, is one great
superiority of Science over Religion, for Science still
bristles with unsolved mysteries, whereas God is the
answer to everything. And, as I have mentioned, it was
those blue lizards which took Norman to Capri in 1888 and
decided his destiny, for his memory will live chiefly in that
land of sirens, even if the sirens now have all been changed
into extraordinary women.

Between 1896 and 1901 Douglas published nothing.
Why? Another point to be investigated. Perhaps service
in the Foreign Office and marriage had something to do
with his silence. Then in 1901 Norman and his wife issued
a book of *Unprofessional Tales* under the pseudonym,
Normyx. His biographer will have to read it, but I am
going to take Norman's advice to me when I asked him
about it, and leave it alone. I should not be surprised if
those unprofessional tales turned out to be amateurish
short stories.

Putting aside *South Wind*, which is unique in his production and, I would claim, in English literature, fiction
was not altogether the right form of expression for
Norman's remarkable gifts. His intellect was too positive,
his interests perhaps over-specialised, and his theories both
of life and of novels too hard-and-fast. His early story
called *Nerinda*, the short stories in *Experiments*, the two

chapters of that abortive novel he wrote at Baalbek in
1928, all show the same lack of the story-teller's art which
mark *In the Beginning* and *They Went* as failures. Everybody
knows (perhaps even from personal experience) how very
easy it is to write bad novels and how very hard and rare it
is to produce a really good one. Yet a writer is to be
judged by his achievements, not by his failures, and to me
South Wind makes up for all the others. It seems to me that
I trace its influence on many of the writers between 1919
and 1939. And yet to my astonishment and chagrin I find
that my younger friends refuse to admire *South Wind* and
even find it tiresome. They enjoy all Douglas's books
except the novels, including *South Wind*. Is this the
perversity of taste which makes one generation utterly
disrelish what its seniors perhaps over-admired? Personally, if you really admire *Siren Land* and *Old Calabria*, I
don't see how you can fail to like *South Wind*, which is in
much the same key of blue.

In the early years of this century Douglas's interests
moved rather away from natural history to archæology
and antiquarian research, if we may judge by the pamphlets
he issued between 1904 and 1907, and later collected in
Capri Materials. These papers were put together from
researches in the libraries of Naples and Cava, the archives
of Capri and the author's own collection of documents.
His books, pamphlets and prints dealing with Capri and its
history eventually included nearly 500 items. It was the
loss of these which, he says, discouraged him from
producing yet another book on Capri. In *Looking Back* he
tells how he first sold his collection of Tunisian palæoliths
and, driven harder by poverty, had to sell his cherished
Capri library. Both were bought by an American lady,
Mrs. Webb, apparently more for the purpose of giving
Norman some money than because she wanted or could

make the slightest use of his collections. This was
generous in Mrs. Webb, who had the sense to see that here
was a man of intellectual powers in real need of money.
He had apparently drawn an income from the Douglas
cotton mills in Vorarlberg until he was going on for forty,
when the income vanished—I never asked or found out
why. He had cut himself off from a career in the Foreign
Office, and at that age a scholarly voluptuary cannot
improvise a profession or trade. Doubtless Mrs. Webb
saw that the only thing to do was to try to tide him over
until he got on his financial feet as a writer, a trade which
needs no apprenticeship, is open to all comers, and in
which really important persons may have masterpieces
written in their name by hirelings picturesquely called
'ghosts'.

But how much did Mrs. Webb give for these collections?
Fifty pounds each; which does not seem very lavish. It
may perhaps have paid for the stones, but it strikes me that
to get those 500 rare Capri items at an average price of two
shillings was a very good bargain indeed. Did such another
collection exist even in public libraries, unless indeed with
Cerio or Axel Munthe? I question whether such a
collection could now be brought together for five hundred
pounds, let alone fifty. And what happened to it? Was it
eventually dispersed or stored in some vast library where
nobody ever looks at it? I can't see that it would be of
much use to people who have never seen Capri: really it
could only be of service to some scholarly exile, like
Norman, who had lived on the island for years. If Mrs.
Webb had been as intelligent as she was wealthy and well-
meaning, I think she would have said:

"My dear Norman, I am very happy to have become the
owner of your remarkable Capri collection, but I am not a
specialist, and can make no real use of them. So while it is

understood that they belong to me I beg that you will continue to retain them until you have finished whatever writings on Capri you have in mind. I should then like to present them to some public library or, if you prefer, to sell them off piecemeal for the benefit of private collectors."

Why didn't she say that or words to that effect? Probably it never occurred to her. And she might have hesitated even if she had thought of it from a not unfounded suspicion that he would have thanked her charmingly, pocketed the cheque, and kept the collection, or perhaps have sold it to someone else. But would that have mattered so much? It is fretting to think that for the sake of a miserable two hundred and fifty dollars we may have lost a good English-language book on Capri. And yet I wonder. Even if he had retained that collection and the leisure for what he flatteringly calls "these gentlemanly studies", would he have written the book after he found that he had been forestalled by Harold Trower's *Book of Capri*? It is true that this book has small literary merit and lacks that flavour of abstruse erudition which Norman hit off so well, but in its modest way Trower's book covers most of the possible Capri topics, which, anyway, were already very hackneyed by then, and he includes Douglas on the *Blue Grotto*. Incidentally, Norman developed a furious vendetta against this man Trower and satirised him virulently in *South Wind*, as I shall have occasion to mention later on. For the moment, I will refer only to one little Capri episode which shows the ridiculous pettiness with which this feud was carried on. In 1900, three Englishmen, including Trower, chartered a yacht to explore the White Grotto. It is true that Trower did not actually enter the grotto, but he was certainly of the party and bore his share of the expense. Norman gives his usually scrupulously accurate account of the transaction, but omits all mention of Trower! (What next!)

Continuing with Douglas's publications and the very slow growth of his literary genius, we come upon the essay on E. A. Poe which was reprinted in *Experiments*. It is surely a noteworthy example of the great latitude permissible in the science of literary criticism when we find two such distinguished men as Norman Douglas and Aldous Huxley differing so widely on the subject of Poe. According to Norman, Edgar Allen Poe was 'a great anti-vulgarian', whereas in his essay on *Vulgarity in Literature* Aldous Huxley picks on Poe as one of the vulgarians of all time. I should have liked to hear them debate it, but for some reason Huxley was never present at our cheerful meals. Perhaps he had heard rumours of those grey truffles. And then Pino does not seem to have been very forthcoming. He was always having to go to some spa to nurse that inefficient liver of his, and one day after he came back from Montecatini he said casually that he had seen a good deal of Huxley. "Come now, sir," said I, "this is an interesting matter; do favour us with it. What did Mr. Huxley say?" "Oh," said Pino indifferently, "Aldous he sit and make remark." And that was all I could get out of him.

Douglas himself counted his entry into the literary world as having occurred with that Poe article, though it was so immensely out-distanced by *The Island of Typhoeus*, which appeared in *The English Review* for February, 1909, that I should much prefer to call that his real *début* in literature. I have that copy of *The English Review* before me now, and a reading of the contributions suggests two reflections. One is that purely as prose, as well as in the expression of a strong personality, this essay of Norman's is far above the other contributors, though they included Conrad, Wells, Granville Barker and Hueffer. The second is that the reading public failed to perceive that a new prose writer of distinction had arisen, just as they failed to support *The English Review*. In addition to those I have mentioned, that number alone contained Yeats, Hauptmann, De la Mare ('Here lies a most beautiful lady'!), Galsworthy and Vernon Lee. All those early numbers are up to the same standard, yet I believe Hueffer and his publisher lost badly on every number, and that the review had to be subsidised when Austin Harrison and Norman Douglas took over as editors. Possibly Masefield's closhy puts and bloody liars put *The English Review* on its feet at last, but it needed such an appeal to the great heart of the nation to achieve that result.

Curious how little Norman says in *Looking Back* (or anywhere else) about his connection with *The English Review*, and I have not been able to find out even how long he worked for it. Here and there he has a bare allusion to the review, asserts that he had to cut down D. H. Lawrence's stories (which I take leave to doubt) and tells us that in spite of his protests and pleas Harrison always kept Flecker's scripts waiting for an unreasonable time. Now I come to think of it, I never heard Norman once mention his *English Review* days. He must have been poor at the time, and perhaps the memory of them was disagreeable. It is another line of enquiry for that biographer.

The *Typhoeus* essay is about Ischia, and one would think it ought to have made an instant hit, at any rate with people who travelled and prided themselves on literary good taste. Here was a combination of qualities at once attractive and original. You had the abstruse, out-of-the-way learning contrasting and blending with Norman's zest for living, that geological and botanical knowledge linking up with his life-long passion for trees and afforestation, his enjoyment of land, sea and sky, the taste for local wines, local

characters, local history, the amused cynical wisdom, the
unabashed hedonism with its laughter at 'religious nonsense', and the grotesquely playful vein of caricature—and
then the sparkles of Voltairean wit: "Vengeance is mine,
said the Jewish god who liked to keep all the good things
to himself."

Typhoeus, I insist, was Douglas at his best and gayest, his
most life-and-laughter-loving; yet to read it quite intact
one must go to that early number of *The English Review*, for
the version in *Summer Islands* is not complete. What can
have happened? Was this one of the seven chapters cut by
the publisher from *Siren Land* as 'too remote from human
interests'? If so, that publisher had weird ideas of what is
and is not humanly interesting. In any case Norman did
not allow the essay to be wholly wasted, but worked pages
and paragraphs into other chapters of the book. I regret
this, because the original essay was so good, and because
this snipping up what was written about Ischia and working
it into essays on other places strikes me as artificial and
factitious. But what were the other omitted chapters?
Perhaps the essay on the Ponza Islands, some of the *Capri
Materials* and some of *Old Calabria*? I should think it highly
unlikely that any of them remained unpublished, but were
used for revamping old work as padding.

In spite of the publisher's intelligent care to keep *Siren
Land* humanly interesting, the publication was a complete
failure and most of the first edition was pulped. Surviving
copies must be rare and expensive. In 1923, twelve years
after this rebuff, *Siren Land* was reprinted, and has since
been widely read.

Beautifully as *Looking Back* is written I don't find in it
either the animation or strength of the earlier books nor so
many memorable passages. A striking paragraph which is
often quoted runs thus:

"I have arrived at a time of life when all men, no matter of what nationality and class, fall into two main divisions: those who value human relationships, and those who value social or financial advancement. The first division enjoys its friends and strives to deserve their love; the second division uses its friends and strives to turn them to profit. The first division are gentlemen; the second division are cads."

Setting aside the 'gentlemen' and 'cads', most people would no doubt agree wholly with these excellent sentiments, though it seems a pity that Norman waited until he was sixty before making the discovery, which I hope he put into practice. And it would be more convincing if later in the same book we did not come on a passage in which he airily remarks that he "used to frequent Mrs. Webb's society, during that impecunious period, mainly in the hope of extracting some money out of her." The two passages seem to me incompatible—you can't frequent friends mainly in the hopes of getting money out of them, and at the same make a lofty boast of 'gentlemanly' feelings because you scorn 'social or financial advancement'.

There is also the striking passage in which he takes leave of his readers. It is about Leydig, a German physiologist, a type of German who must now be nearly, if not wholly, extinct since, like Goethe, he thought that 'this national nonsense' of war hatreds should not 'intrude into the scholar's study'. The collapse of this civilised view and its supersession by a deliberate policy of inculcating political and nationalist prejudices and hates give some indication of post-war degradation—genuine culture can no more survive under blatant demagogues than under criminal tyrants. But here is what Douglas wrote of Leydig:

F

"His emphasis on individuality fell on fertile soil. He supplied me with a formula for avoiding those flat lands of life where men absorb each others' habits and opinions to such an extent that nothing is left save a herd of flurried automata."

These are brave words, and the vivid phrase, 'flurried automata', seems an even more accurate description of the mass-conditioned, propaganda-scared crowds than it was in 1932. But I wonder whether Norman was so successful in avoiding 'the flat lands of life' as this paragraph and other remarks imply? Lawrence's bitter lapidary phrase that Douglas was "very much at an end of everything" was true, and at any rate in those days of which I am writing he had spells of dreadful ennui. He let drop the fact that at times he spent much of his morning sitting down with his eyes closed and his head leaning against the wall because there was nothing he wanted to do. At another time, more hopefully, he was suggesting that if somebody would stand him half a bottle of vintage champagne every morning about eleven he might be able to do some writing. It is a remedy for disinclination to work which I should think many people would not be averse from trying. By 1932 all his early scientific and antiquarian interests were dead, except by way of reminiscence. He had been a musician, and probably a better one than most people supposed, as he had studied with Rubinstein, but except for his playing some records of Brahms and Rubinstein on Pino's gramophone, I don't remember that he had kept any trace of his former enthusiasms. I never saw him at the symphony concerts in Florence or at the more select concerts of chamber-music at the Pitti palace. We did once lure him to the opera, but the piece was changed to *Manon*, and he evaporated from the *loge* before the end of the first act—a trick of his on occasions which I used to think rather rude when there were women present, especially in a professional gentleman. He said he had long ago taken a vow never to enter a church, and certainly to my personal knowledge neither he nor Pino ever entered one, except that Pino did once or twice on our Sicilian trip. Norman inveighed so vehemently against the 'Cinquecento' nonsense of art (meaning the Uffizi, Pitti and church paintings of Florence!) that one had to sneak off to see them. I cannot remember that the inventor of the Locri Faun ever said anything interesting about ancient sculpture, or indeed ever mentioned the topic. He seemed to have given up reading even, and took little interest in contemporary literature—for which indeed he can hardly be blamed. He must have kept some interest in Homeric studies, for I still remember winning a small bet from him by finding in a Toulon bookshop a copy of Sénateur Bérard's commentary on the *Odyssey*, which Norman bought at once.

Now, it may be that my memory is at fault, or that I was unfortunate, and that he talked to others on these topics and not to me. It is true that Pino was very often with us, and that for some reason he was usually in such a very anti-culture mood that we were forced away from any such subjects.

4

I HAVE been wondering how long my first experience of Pinorman in Florence lasted. Certainly I should have been very slow if I had not discovered the real Pino by Christmas 1930, especially after that Christmas Eve display in the Duomo. But when did Norman return from his painful tooth operation in Paris? So unreliable is memory in such matters that I should have said confidently that he was not in Florence until about the middle of January 1931. Yet I have turned up that letter from Charles, dated 28th December, 1930, saying he had just received "a letter from Douglas which rejoiced me greatly, saying that he was returning to Florence at once and hoping that he'd catch you before you were off again." I have also just discovered, what I had completely forgotten, that Norman gave me a copy of *Experiments*, which I find inscribed: "To Richard Aldington from Norman Douglas, 10 Jan 1931". I must have told him before that date that I had not read *Experiments*, and, of course, he wanted me to read his anti-Lawrence Magnus pamphlet. This makes me wonder whether that fearful test of Sor Giovanni's grey truffles in cheese may have been a Scottish New Year's Eve celebration! I don't remember; nor do I remember whether on that occasion Reggie Turner was there, or whether it was another when he had an acid, spinsterish bicker with Norman about those truffles—whereupon, of course, it became a point of honour with Norman's adherents 'to lap them up' and say they were delicious. Reggie could never forgive me for preferring Norman's and Lawrence's books to his. With a wave of the hand, which I always felt must have been copied from Oscar, and that strange 'flapping' of his eyelids due to some small eye trouble he refused to have treated, he would condole with me on belonging to a dull generation—'you haven't our wit, our sparkle.' I still have a feeling not of remorse, but of useless pain, when I remember that Reggie brought me two of his books to read, so hopefully, and then when he found I could not praise them took them silently away. Reggie, who had more than one disability, was so vulnerable one hated to hurt him. I think Norman was right when he said Reggie ought not to have been in Florence but in Kensington handing round the tea cakes.

The spring came and with it a temporary end to our laughter and talk and lunches and dinners, which were far from being the 'muck' Norman grumbled that they were. Norman began to fret about the tourists pouring into the town and that seemed to affect Pino's nerves. One reason we went to Fusi's was that it looked too dirty and the wine was too good, for foreigners. Then in an evil moment the waiter at Fusi's made the fearful blunder of saying something to Pino in pidgin English, which he had evidently been studying in the hope of fleecing wor-shippers at the art shrines of Florence. Let us say his name was Arturo. Anyway, Pino spoke with a ferocious calm as he uttered in Italian the memorable words: "Arturo, if you ever speak to me in English again I'll kick your backside."

Obviously, it was time to separate until another autumn swept the town comparatively clear and we might, if we chose, renew our convivialities. By May I was installed for the summer in a villa on the Côte des Maures, and Norman and Pino evidently went to Capri for a time, though Norman's restlessness soon brought them back again. One or two letters have somehow survived, and the earliest is from Pino and dated 13th May, 1931:

"My dear Richard and all,
Just back from Capri. I went to see Norman there, we had a lovely week there. Stopped in Rome and saw a magnificent procession of a Greek Madonna with 20 cardinals following, Georgie was kneeling down asking 'perdono' and the Madonna said: 'go my dear girl you will be a great success in the world you will walk all over the world and never stop at the station stalls of Messrs W. H. Smith and Sons Ltd.' I was rather surprise the Madonna knew English and Messrs Smith and Sons Ltd.
Pity Charles did not pass through Florence. I am please he is happy about Georgie. . . . I do miss all of you, I certainly hope to come to Canadel, is it far from Bandol? I will write soon a longer letter. Love to all my dearest

ever,

Pino."

This rather unintelligible fooling about the Madonna, Georgie and W. H. Smith was Pino's fun at the expense of one of Charles's authors whose books were refused for sale on the pretence of 'obscenity'. Looking over these letters from Charles and other publisher friends in England, I find that when their authors' books were not being 'banned by the libraries' as obscene the publishers were being prosecuted for libel on pretexts so frivolous that one can have nothing but contempt for a legal organisation which permitted them. I remember Charles telling me that he was startled, though not surprised, to receive a lawyer's letter one morning threatening libel proceedings, heavy damages, &c., because a recently-published book had described Mr. X (now defunct) as an 'anti-Semite'. After looking up the text Charles wrote back politely, pointing out that his author had said Mr. X was 'an anti-anti-Semite'. Between them these two little rackets nicely achieved their purpose of suppressing authors who happened to displease the more backward sections of the community and of causing financial loss to both authors and publishers. As I shall mention later, they even reached out after Pino in Florence but were fortunately defeated.

Norman's letter was written after they returned from Capri, on 25th May, and is on paper headed 'c/o Thomas Cook, Via Tornabuoni, Florence', which he then used as his permanent address. Why did he not have letters delivered to his flat? Well, it was on the top floor, which meant he would have had to have a private letter-box at the downstairs entrance, from which letters might have been stolen. As parcels would either be brought up (which meant a tip) or held for collection at the post office, Cook's was obviously better. And then if he went off on a sudden impulse he hadn't to bother about letters. Finally, if he didn't want to be troubled with letters for a few days he could secure complete immunity by the simple process of not collecting them at Cook's. All this he propounded with relish while walking, and it strikes me as characteristic that he gave so much attention to the details of the problem.

This letter runs:

25 May, 1931

"My dear Richard,
Please excuse a miserable scrawl in reply to your

truly noble epistle of the 18th. I am considerably fussed just now—very considerably!

I should love to come and see you for a moment one of these days. It is possible that I may go in your direction, but only for a week or so, in a short time; if so, I'll drop you a line. Hotel, of course. Wouldn't dream of putting you out.

Pino flourishes under Reggie's supervision. Now that we live in the same house, we don't see as much of each other as we used to do. XYZ have been here, and Y read some poems in somebody's palazzo, for which he was offered, and *took*, £60. That is the only social news I can think of, except that I had my hair cut two days ago.

Ever so much love to B.
Yours always
Norman."

There are one or two remarks in that letter which are well worth examination—curious how revealing even a casual note like this may be. At that time I had not yet realised that Norman, like most possessive people, was jealous, especially of anyone with whom Pino struck up a friendship and who seemed likely to take him away from his usual waiting on Norman's whims and entertaining his boredom. I think I unintentionally did the wrong thing by taking Pino on that long motor trip without Norman in 1932, and it would not surprise me if he was also a little jealous of Charles. But Charles was a transient and always had to return to his office, and I never spent more than a few months at a time in Florence. Reggie lived in Florence, was devoted to Pino, and also had an old man's boredom, which Pino's vitality and stories drove away. There was thus a competition between the two of them,

and for a considerable time Norman was easily the more
powerful attraction. But Reggie had considerable tenacity,
and just about this time played a trump card which beat
Norman. He allowed Pino to learn or told him that all
his money had been willed to Pino, and it is a fact that in
1938 Pino did inherit about £20,000 from his friend.

Any poor man would be glad to inherit £20,000, but I
think that to poor Italians such a gift of the gods has a
particular glamour—it pleases their mystical love of money
and that sense of splendour they have, while of course it is
so very unlikely to happen. I think all these motives came
into play with Pino, but he had additional reasons for
exultation. He had insensibly got into a way of living
which, while far from luxurious or extravagant, was more
and more beyond his income as a bookseller, which
dwindled as the great slump deepened. The interest on
that sum would enable him to live comfortably in Florence,
and the promise of it removed any fears he may have had
about his old age. Therefore, although Pino would
certainly have preferred to be with Norman, he felt he had
to spend a good deal of time with Reggie, and if he showed
any real signs of neglect Reggie had only to give a display
of what Samuel Butler called 'will shaking' to bring him to
order at once.

Occasionally this led to little comedies in which,
without realising it at the time, I suspect I was used by
Norman as an unconscious tool to tempt Pino away from
some engagement with Reggie. Something of this sort
would happen. Norman would drop in at the Santa Croce
flat or catch me on my afternoon's walk with his usual
"Hello, Chawly." After some talk he would say:

"I found out from Betti this morning that they've got
cinghiale to-night. We might dine there all four of us,
just for a change. Ha! Always the same muck. But I'll

see they have chocolate and vinegar sauce. What about it?"

Naturally I would say "Yes", and then he would go on:

"I haven't seen Pino today, and I simply must spend the afternoon and evening at the University Library. You pick up Pino, and we'll meet at Betti's—seven-thirty sharp."

Well, I would then proceed to Lungarno delle Grazie, and find Pino asleep over his catalogue or meditating some of his hair-raisingly scandalous stories about the visiting English who were too respectable by half. "Norman wants us to eat *cinghiale* at Betti's to-night," I would say presently. "Will you pick us up about seven?"

At moments of perplexity Pino produced a piece of acting which is hard to describe. He would shrug his shoulders, with his arms and hands lifted in supplication, and at the same cower or almost cringe, like Shylock deprecating the Doge's wrath.

"I *can* not, I *can* not."

"Why not?"

"*Reggie!* He say I must dine at home with him in Viale Milton tonight, and I bet he give me *lemb chop*."

Words in italics were delivered with an emphasis print cannot convey. The history of the lamb chops and the disgrace attached to them was known to me. Reggie, it seemed, had once given lunch to Pino and Frank Harris at Nice and served lamb chops, whereupon Harris had jeered at this meanness until "Reggie, he blink like mad."

"Oh, well. Surely he can spare you for one evening. When I saw Norman he seemed to be in very good form, but it won't be real fun unless you're there."

Then of course Pino's mind would be the scene of one of those conflicts the playwrights tell us about, Pino struggling between fear of compromising his all-important heritage from Reggie and longing to have a merry evening with Norman, instead of hearing what Robbie said to Bosie when Oscar was at Dieppe, for about the hundredth time. At this point Pino would say in abject misery:

"Shall ve have some vine?"

Sometimes the 'vine' settled it in our favour, sometimes he might come part way to the restaurant and then he would suddenly think how awful it would be if Reggie left all his money to his servants, and rush off in a taxi to Viale Milton.

"Where's Pino?" Norman would ask when he failed to arrive.

"I'm sorry, but he had engaged to dine with Reggie."

"Umph."

Pino chafed and rebelled against this servitude to Reggie's will as he did from time to time against Norman's domination. He was particularly exasperated by the neat and respectable comfort of Reggie's flat, which he said was 'si-si'—meant to be French, chi-chi. His exasperation sometimes goaded him to outrageous protests. The example I remember best happened when Frere was in Florence in 1932. At the same time the grown-up daughter of an old friend of Norman's arrived, and it was arranged that we should all go to Reggie's to meet her. Reggie had recently acquired a handsome radio and could think of nothing better to entertain us than to turn it on, though he must have known that Norman hated it. Dance music coming over suggested to some ill-inspired person that we should dance. If only there had been present a Savoyard with a drum and a stick, you could not have asked for a more life-like representation of dancing bears. Came the moment when Frere had to dance with the guest, and as they could both dance well their superiority was so obvious that everyone else stopped to watch appreciatively.

Pino was the exception, obviously extremely jealous of all this glory going to a publisher who had not risen to the typographical splendours of the Lungarno Series.

After two or three efforts to jeer the dancers down, and finding nobody paid any attention to him, he went off in a huff; and I thought he had gone to have a glass of Chianti with Reggie's servants as he sometimes did when the 'si-si' got to be too much for him. Far from it. We had forgotten about him, when suddenly he flung the door open and pranced into the room waving his arms and announcing he was Salome, stark naked except for Reggie's dressing-gown and some sort of grotesque wreath round his head. For a minute or two we were amused, though I don't think anyone realised at the time— at least I didn't—that this was intended as a crushing satire on our two elegant dancers. Then it got beyond a joke. Not only was Pino exposing himself in an indecent way, but was making threatening gestures and uttering insults to the girl, who was surprised and indignant, and a little frightened by this monstrous apparition. Reggie was clucking like an outraged hen, Frere saw he had better not interfere, and at last Norman and I half-persuaded, half-dragged Pino into Reggie's dressing-room. Once there all Pino's rage and energy suddenly left him under the realisation that he had made a fool of himself, angered Reggie and insulted Norman's guest. He collapsed on a couch and sat in silent misery mournfully holding his penis.

Pino's next rebellion against Reggie—at least that I witnessed—seems insignificant in comparison. This was at one of Reggie's tea parties, where he seemed very happy playing the part of host, seeing that tea and English bread-and-butter and cakes were served to his guests sitting or standing in little groups in his *salone*, 'blinking his eyes like mad' as he paid compliments to the women and was sparkling and witty to the men. All this completely bore out the diagnosis of Norman (who was not there—catch him!) that Reggie would have been happiest in a land of many tea parties and not where they were rare and seasonal. But it was extremely distasteful to Pino, who (as unjustly as if he had been a Communist) looked on this innocent scene as bourgeois pretentiousness and sickening snobbery. After a rather lengthy visit to the kitchen, he came back and began trying to incite me by denouncing Reggie (*"Look* at him—vot a cretin! Naw, my dear boy, you cannot like such a —— as Reggie" and so forth), with ominous threats of what he'd like to do to such 'si-si'. I managed to draw him off the main stage to a terrace roof-garden Reggie had arranged with the taste such spinsterish men often have, including two large pots with lemon trees covered with fruit, 'really quite a Crivelli touch,' as they would say in Florence. But Pino was not to be appeased by my praise of Reggie as an arranger of flowers and plants. It only increased his bile, until in an agony of disapprobation of 'si-si' he suddenly sprang away and before I could move or speak bit a large piece out of each of three of the most conspicuous and decorative lemons—entirely ruining the effect of Reggie's carefully thought out scheme of fruit and foliage decoration. I cannot remember what denunciations of 'si-si' then followed, and perhaps it is just as well.

Coming back to that letter from Norman last quoted—what did he mean by that sentence: "I am considerably fussed just now—very considerably!" I have no idea, but I can't help suspecting that he may have been involved in one of his many scrapes with outraged parents or the police which arose from his peculiar habits. He was quite literally *paiderastes*, a lover of boys, and it is falsifying his

whole existence to ignore it. In the late nineteenth and
twentieth centuries he behaved in Western Europe as if he
were living in Eastern Mediterranean countries at some
period between the age of Plato and that of Hadrian. The
Musa Puerilis of Strato was entirely in his line, and Norman
—who constantly betrays this taste to a careful reader—
reveals it clearly enough when he mentions an epigram of
Rufinus as expressing a "sudden and *almost incredible* change
in his erotic tastes". The gist of the epigram is that
Rufinus no longer 'raves about boys' but is 'mad about
women'—a reversal of tastes Norman thought almost
incredible. No wonder he was sometimes 'very considerably fussed'! My inability to feel the slightest
sympathy with this proclivity was, I think, one of several
reasons for later misunderstandings.

My next document is a fragment of another letter, dated
27th September, 1931, on the Cook's, Florence, note-
paper: \

"I suppose you are in town by this time? If so, give
my love to B. and to Charles and Frere. I'm just off
somewhere south; haven't yet made up my mind, but
probably Calabria.

"Pino can't come, too busy! Which is absurd. I
must get away from this howl about money, makes me
sick.

Yours ever,

Norman."

There is another example of Pino's backing away from
Norman to stay near Reggie's will. I don't see how Pino
could possibly have been really busy, for his book trade
must have shrunk to nothing under the prolonged
American depression and, at this time, the British

suspension of gold payments, to which Norman's letters refers. On his return from Calabria, Norman wrote me again, on the 20th October, 1931:

"My dear Richard,

I have just got back from the wilds to find waiting for me two pleasant surprises, namely, B.'s snuff and her charming letter, for which please thank her ever so much—highly appreciated both of them. Still knocked-up with the mountain scrambles and uneatable food and non-existing ——-houses of Calabria. Next time you are in these parts you really must go to Calabria; just make a note of that. By the way, Pino tells me you may be coming here later on. Do try to manage it. We'll find you a room or a palazzo, whichever you want. Much love to B.

Yours ever,

N.D."

I suppose all his English friends at some time or other sent or took him packets of snuff. He always carried a snuff-box, and the only gift he ever made me, apart from his books (which I always reviewed if possible) was a little snuff-box, in which was afterwards inserted a piece of Greek pottery I picked up in the ruins of Selinunte. There were two kinds of snuff he favoured in my time, though I have forgotten what they were called—one was black and highly scented, the other looked like curry powder—and they could only be bought from Fribourg and Treyer in the Haymarket. I don't know where he picked up this habit, but I believe he found a snuff-box useful in making friends among peasants in remote countries. He liked it, also, because it belonged to the habits of an older, less frenzied world.

I had no intention of remaining in England even if the pound went to zero, and started off before the thousands of other European residents who had hastened back on the news of the devalued pound had found courage to start off again. What attracted many of them abroad was not the life of Europe but a rate of exchange favourable to them. The drive back to Florence was memorable. There were few English passengers and practically no other car on the Channel boat, and there were hardly any of the G.B. cars which in those years had been everywhere on the French main roads. What this meant to the hotel and restaurant keepers may be easily imagined. How eagerly they looked for the return of the English may be guessed from this little episode. On our way to Vintimiglia and Italy, we dined in Cannes at what was then Oscar's (it has moved and changed proprietors since the 1939-45 War), and it seems to me we were the only guests. All the same, great care was taken with the menu, and, with the liqueurs, the patron came to the table and supposed politely that we were on our way back to England? On the contrary, we had just come from England, and were on our way to Italy. He was quite overwhelmed. "*Vous venez d'Angleterre!*" he kept repeating happily. Evidently he looked upon us as the first swallows of a new and profitable spring, harbingers of pluckable droves. When we left he absolutely insisted on giving us a bottle of old brandy, as a kind of prize, I suppose, for bringing good news. It is the only time I was ever tipped by a restaurateur, though his kin have had many tips from me.

Before leaving England I had arranged with Charles that he should take a holiday early in 1932, and that we would drive him and Pino through Norman's Old Calabria and round the 3,000 miles of motoring roads which then existed in Sicily. I had come to know this best of friends

by the purest chance. The American publisher of my
novel, *Death of a Hero*, asked me as a favour to offer it first
to Chatto's, because he wanted to stand well with them
and thought the book might succeed. It was read by
Charles, who liked it well enough, and through meetings
in Paris, Venice and London we had become great friends.
I still remember, with a touch of shame, our first meeting
in England, when he invited us to dine with him at
Boulestin's. By that time I had been so long abroad and so
much in the bohemian world that I had forgotten the
English fuss about evening dress, and went in the dark
lounge suit which is the right thing at night in most
Continental restaurants. To my horror Charles was there
in tails, white tie and white waistcoat. It was characteristic of him that it was he who apologised most
sincerely for *his* mistake and wouldn't hear of it being
mine.

Charles was a shy and reserved man, gentle and almost
hesitant in manner, often silent, with a very clear complexion and benevolent expression. With his gold-
rimmed glasses and bald head and kindliness he had some
resemblance to Mr. Pickwick. From my experience I
should say that, without boasting of it, or perhaps even
being conscious of it, he was most decidedly one of those
who 'value human relationships' for their own sake and
not for 'social or financial advantage'. We have given up
praising people for being good or virtuous men, but if I
were asked to name a really 'good' man I have known I
should at once say "Charles". He became for me a kind of
human touchstone, and if people failed to recognise
Charles's qualities underneath that gentle reserve I
mistrusted them. They talk of Scots being mean, though
I've seldom found it so, but with Charles the great
difficulty was to restrain his lavish hospitality and

G

generosity. His kindness was genuine and disinterested.
He was a scholar, particularly devoted to Greek studies,
yet enthusiastic for some modern authors (not the least
meritorious of them, I should say, judging from his list)
and in his quiet way a very able business man as well as a
good designer of books. He was unmarried, and in spite of
his amiable qualities rather a lonely man, living in lodgings
in Earl's Terrace, Kensington, in a chaos of books, boxes
of cigars, wines, and pictures by Wyndham Lewis. Yet in
the depth of winter I discovered he was 'nursing' a cold
in a bleak and gruesome London bedroom without a fire,
and it was only after a lot of unnecessary argument that he
yielded to entreaties and had a frugal gas-fire put in. I
suppose that was the Scot.

He was an Oriel man, and I think took fairly high
honours in classics. One strange result of this Oxford
residence, most remarkable in a man so kind and un-
vindictive, was that he took a very strong dislike to
Shadwell, Pater's friend, in Charles's day the Provost; and
this dislike was so strong that it included Walter Pater, on
whose behalf Charles would not hear a word of praise.
He had very much wanted to write, but, with an unusual
modesty characteristic of him, decided that he must do
the next best thing and publish the authors he liked. This
frustrated ambition made him take a curious pleasure in
being admitted to a writer's workshop to watch the
hopeless struggle. He liked to have a novel sent him
chapter by chapter, to watch it develop, and to col-
laborate with encouragement, suggestions and gentle but
shrewd criticisms. His patience and enthusiasm seemed
inexhaustible, and though some might think his praise too
generous, his hints and diffident suggestions were very
valuable and nearly always right. It was worth working
hard to try to please him, and it is not every London

publisher who can instantly set you right in a misquotation from La Fontaine and run through a version of Euripides with the original before him making amendments and suggestions. He had a great regard for T. F. Powys and (at one time) for Wyndham Lewis, but I think his greatest admiration was for Norman Douglas, and that Pino was perhaps the person whose company gave him most amusement.

That trip very nearly had to be postponed, partly (I think) because of Norman's convivial habits. One sunny winter afternoon I went for a brisk walk, without overcoat, meaning to keep in the sun along the Arno and be back before the evening cold. Coming home, I ran into Norman in overcoat and muffler near the Loggia dei Lanzi. "Hello, Chawley! Where have you been? Brisk walk, eh? Quite right. What you need now is a *mescità*, two of them. Got to get back? Nonsense. What next!" *Mescità* is Florentine for a glass of wine, and he insisted on my coming into a wine-shop he knew—"muck, of course, but what can you expect?" To sit in a dirty, unwarmed, draughty wine-shop off a chilly sunless street about four in the afternoon drinking cold raw Chianti is not my idea of pleasure, and sitting there after being warmed from my walk I got very chilled. In that state of lowered resistance I picked up a throat malady called Vincent's angina. I was really rather ill, and Frieda Lawrence, who was in Firenze at the time, cheered everyone up by remarking in her optimistic way that I looked very much as Lorenzo did just before he died.

Consequently, I started out for Sicily not really strong enough to be responsible for getting the party over rough roads and mountain passes, sometimes in bad weather, in a country where garages and even petrol pumps were few, and spares difficult to find. Norman laughed at us sardonically—we were starting off far too early in the year and were bound to run into snow. He was quite right. The very day we left Florence, the mild sunny winter changed to snowy, thunderous spring. We were not surprised to find snow on Vesuvius, but it was a shock to drive through Salerno in a snowstorm. In spite of which I never had a better and more entertaining car trip. Pino gave us a good start. As we drove out of Florence on the Siena road I asked him at which hotel he would like to put up that night in Rome. "Hotel des Prongs," said he. I had never heard of it, and asked in what street. "Piazza di Spagna," said Pino. Now, in the 1920s I had lived a good deal in Rome, and thought I knew almost every building in the Piazza. . . . "Ah, Hotel des Princes!" I exclaimed, and I can still hear Charles's smothered spasms of laughter. Of course, Pino was indispensable to the journey not only for his own sake but because in those out-of-the-way places a native Italian was essential to do the talking, although down there Pino himself was a *forestiere*. He certainly did his best to help us in every way, and he conceived it to be his duty always to investigate and report on the sanitary arrangements, which, as Norman was never tired of pointing out, are always primitive and sometimes non-existent. In order to make his report without going into squalid details (and also, no doubt, to poke fun at Charles and me for our 'Cinquecento' proclivities) he adopted a symbolical method of classifying them according to Italian art schools, such as 'Quattrocento, scuola di Botticelli' or 'Trecento, Taddeo Gaddi'. Soon he returned from an investigation in some out-of-the-way town with a look of baffled consternation: "My gawd, zhis vun is *Etrusco*!"

The best impression of the pleasure we had on the trip, in spite of the difficulties and discomforts, is given by two

letters from Charles written when he had got back to
England. He had left us at Reggio to return by train, while
we went on to Cotrone, and then back by easy stages to
Florence.

24.3.32

"Dearest Richard,

Your cable from Bagnara was waiting for me, and this
evening there is a whole flight of cards from Reggio and
Bagnara. I wish I could retaliate properly, but I got off
only at Rome and Paris. Since then—what? Romolina
was a travelling paradise, but where are you all now?
I have been utterly lost since I woke to consciousness
on Monday morning somewhere near Naples. It was
excruciating to see the places flick by—Formia, Monte
Massico, the Marshes, the Alban Hills. I sang Pino's
little ditty* to myself when we passed Livorno. But
France put so many miles behind me that I felt I never
wanted to see it again, save in a southward-bound
express, at night. I was thinking of you all continuously, conjecturing your position with the aid of
Baedeker's exiguous maps, and going back again and
again to what we had done and seen, and blessing and
loving you all. Such a time as I had I could never have
imagined.

How I miss you, and how I long to have been with
you at Bagnara, and to be with you now—not too near
Florence, I hope, but elegantly looping road-curves
under a bright and tender sun or quaffing some real
wine round a satisfying bowl of triglie [i.e. red mullet]
or capretto [i.e. kid]. What a time you gave me. I can
never thank you enough, and what would we have done
without your stout and obstinate driving I really don't

* I think this must be 'Il molino . .

know—and your directing mind and B.'s pots and pans* and darling Pino and all the good cheer. We were a marvellous party, though I blush when I think over my own little doings. What *did* Charles do? He just enjoyed himself, sometimes a trifle raptly, but he did enjoy himself as much as any. . . . Anyone would like to go round Sicily in a car, but I was the only one who went with you and B. and Pino, who also wouldn't have been there if it hadn't been for you. . . ."

A week later Charles was still full of our doings and of regrets at being back in London:

31.3.32

"Dearest Richard,

It is very bloody being back in this dump of chaos and frayed ends. You feel like one of those tickers at a club that registers the most fantastic variorum of idiotic events, one on the heels of another, no connection, no reason. And the dear April showers sprinkle us spasmodically. And yellow daffodils are everywhere. Your postcards and rhymes and staggering letters have been a great leg-up. How I wish I had been with you to sample the Cirò! Better than Pellaro? I would be surprised at no excellence in that delectable land. Frere dined me last night, and I told him of some of the doings, but when I look back upon what I said, I see I can't have given him the notion of even a millionth part of the glorious time we had. (I must get hold of him again soon.) What a time! I've thought of it continually. You were all darlings—and but for the car and your driving vot *could* we have done? I hope you got back to Florence without any more bursts or accidents.

* He means the picnic things.

What hops you did. I'd dearly love to have sped past
Campo Tenese at 50 m.p.h. I hope too that the flat is
as you left it, and now full of warm sun—a lovely flat; I
shall always remember it and my stay there (luridly as
my visit began,* but I trust I appeared funny rather than
tragic.) *Will* you be coming here this summer? It
seems so 'FUNNY' for day and day to pass, and no seeing
you. The £ has soared to 73. Why aren't I with
you? . . .

You may make all the allowances you choose for the
praise of an over-generous and lonely man, but you can
hardly say that he had not spent a happy month in congenial company, seeing much of interest, and coming on
many amusing episodes enlivened by Pino's fun. And Pino
also expressed great pleasure in his own style. Of course,
our main objective was Sicily, which Charles and Pino had
never seen, while I had been there twice, and not Norman's
Calabria, which in those days was better explored by mule
or on foot than by car. From what I saw of Calabria (and
by this I mean more than the modern province and include
all that area of South Italy Norman calls Old Calabria) I
should say it is a better country to read and write about
than to linger in for pleasure. I am very glad to have seen
it, not only for its classical memories, but because I can
now visualise the landscape and villages and people which
occupy such excellent and inexhaustible books as Ramage's
Nooks and Byways of Italy, Gissing's *By the Ionian Sea*,
Lenormant's *La Grande Grèce* and, best of all, Norman
Douglas's *Old Calabria*.

Earthquakes and wars, harryings of Saracens and Turks,
religious fanatics, deforestation, tyrants, brigands have
made almost total destruction of all that men created here

* A "disturbo".

and have obliterated or basely degraded their descendants. What remains of the brilliant city-states of Magna Græcia? —Croton is a squalid burg of poor people, Locri is a name, the very site of splendid Sybaris is lost. What come ye here for to see? What we found were dirty villages which stank, earthquake-shattered ruins, mere dens of dwellings, a neglected and barbarous population, among which such towns as Catanzaro, Cosenza and even Castrovillari stand as most worthy exceptions—towns which in northern Italy would attract little attention. The landscape is wild enough and often beautiful, but so far as monuments of the great past are concerned you must see nearly all of them with the eyes of historical memory and take them on trust. On your map you see a name great in history; in fact you see a desolate marsh or a few shapeless broken stones or a malaria-smitten village, just as in old London you are incited to admiration for sooty plaques, once blue and white, indicating that such and such a noble building or famous monument once stood on the site of these dingy offices. And at least in London is the surge of life. Though no believer in a paradise of social justice I can never achieve Norman's robust indifference to human poverty and misery. Pino was very anxious that we should not miss Spezzano Albanese (we couldn't, as the only possible road went through it), saying: "Norman have written about it." I remember driving through a dingy street of squalor and stench, with glimpses of a throng of pallid, unfed people in dirty clothes. They are said to be descendants of Albanians who fled from the Turks, and I found that what Norman had written of them was that an "epidemic of cholera" would "work wonders" for the town!

One of the few picturesque survivals in those days were the local costumes, which still lingered on in the remoter places, and—unfortunately much more rarely but more wonderfully—some lingering traces of great physical beauty in the people. This was the case in Tiriolo, which then retained its costume, and where a few of the youngest men and women were really handsome, tall and well-built, with oval faces, dark hair and eyes, and well-shaped mouths. Alas! Tiriolo was a town of dreadful dens, where the young children must die like falling leaves in autumn, and the beauty of the few that survive is soon destroyed by cruel hard toil or child-bearing. They are said to be the last descendants of the Bruttii, who held that land before the Romans arrived in their destructive liberation.

Certainly that, and much else in Old Calabria, were worth coming to experience, but to see it we had to put up with very 'plain' hotels and sometimes a real penury of food—a contrast even to Sicily. Ramage made his journey on foot in 1828, and says that, after the villages where he had stayed since leaving Salerno, there was "more appearance of comfort" in Sapri than anywhere he had yet seen. Our fare there was well enough—spaghetti, pieces of kid roasted on metal skewers, and goat's cheese—but we discovered the place was so poor that the inn had only two bottles of wine, and when we tried to get a little milk at breakfast to dilute that liquid liquorice there called coffee, we were told that only one litre had come in that morning, and it had gone not to children but to the priest. Buffalo, which is sometimes served in those parts, is uneatable, but there seemed no other meat save kid. Pino and Charles used to go off and forage for our picnic lunch while I got the car ready. I seem to remember that on one occasion all they could find was olives, buffalo-milk cheese (good), raw broad-beans, poor bread and poorer wine. Another day we greeted Pino as a benefactor when he managed to wheedle some smoked eel out of an old woman. Yet you couldn't tell. The best spaghetti any of us had ever eaten was served to us at Palmi (Pino tried in vain to get the recipe), while Cotrone, which nearly killed Gissing with its penury, provided a clean hotel, an excellent dinner and almost the best wine we found—and though some of the Calabrian wines are awful, there are some which are exceptionally good.

Charles, I think, enjoyed it more than any of us, partly because it was so complete a change from his humdrum life in London, partly because his classical scholarship gave him a far greater knowledge of the history and associations. I recollect two occasions when he chose inappropriate moments to arouse my enthusiasm for antiquity by telling me we were near or approaching the site of a town where a great writer of ancient Greece had died. One was in Calabria, when I was very tired, on a seemingly endless mountain road which twisted without respite, was narrow and with a precipice I had to skirt in that awkward gloom between twilight and dark. He leaned forward and said in his gentle voice: "Herodotus died here, Richard." I very nearly said "Damn Herodotus." As a matter of fact, for once Charles was not quite accurate. Thurii, if I am not blundering, was near the site of Sybaris, and while Charles was with us we were never within fifteen miles of it. The other occasion was on the desolate but lovely south coast of Sicily. I could see a small town ahead and was praying I could get there in time—there was a sad lack of pull in the engine and I could feel by the sideways tug on the steering-wheel that my left front tyre was deflating. Charles chose this moment to remind me that this was Gela, where Æschylus died, and they afterwards invented that silly story of the eagle dropping a tortoise on his bald pate.

After Norman's *Old Calabria* and the Frenchman with the similar-sounding name of Lenormant, the most enjoyable book on Old Calabria is Ramage's, and I am happy to express my gratitude to Norman for writing the best of them and introducing me to the two others. Ramage, I think, is not mentioned in *Old Calabria*, but there are some sage remarks about him in *Alone*. He, like Norman, was a formidably erudite Scot, but I take leave to doubt whether he really carried in his memory all those classical texts which he invariably quotes about the place he happens to be studying. I have it in mind that as long ago as the time of Addison there was a compilation made of all such quotations for the use of travellers with a classical education—and what others should ever be allowed to make the grand tour? Norman mentions, but I think does not quote in full, Ramage's description of his equipment for his formidable walking tour:

"I have a white merino frock-coat, well furnished with capacious pockets, into which I have stuffed my maps and note-books; nankeen trousers, a large-brimmed straw hat, white shoes and an umbrella . . ."

This was the umbrella with which, being awakened by what he thought were cut-throats in some remote *locanda*, he prepared to defend his life, as with a puissant pike. Norman reflects on the superstitious peasant dislike for such clothes, but think of what such a costume must have looked like after a few days of roughing it on foot in Old Calabria, fording streams, sleeping fully clothed in buggy beds, lying down under trees, being soaked in thunderstorms! They started out white, and ended up looking like the 'rags of an Irish beggar', clothed in which Ramage serenely presented to local nobles the letters of introduction he had received in Naples from the Prince of Satriano, Duca di Filangieri! Now, I can entirely go along

with Norman in his love for such 'gentlemanly freaks', as
he calls them, but I must say I draw the line at his hideous
Dorftrottels, deaf-mutes, and so forth, as well as at the
problematic pleasures of unkempt cemeteries, and of
watching urchins bloodily decapitating fowls for the hotel
dinner he was going to eat. It is well to have strong
nerves and not to be squeamish, but need one *enjoy* such
things?

I once asked Norman point-blank how long he had been
in writing *Old Calabria*, and in that knock-'em-flat crisp
manner of his he snapped:

"Thirty years!"

Now what on earth made him say such a silly thing?
Since the book was first published in 1915 that figure,
taken literally, would mean that he had begun it in 1885,
three years before he ever entered Italy, and on his own
showing he was never in Old Calabria until 1907. I
suppose you could say that he dated it from the very
beginning of his study of Italian in Karlsruhe, but on that
basis Voltaire could have claimed he had been over sixty
years writing his last tragedy of *Irène*. *Old Calabria* is
obviously a sequel to *Siren Land* and almost certainly
contains some of its rejected material. In *Late Harvest* he
says the writing of *Old Calabria* occupied "a good many
years". Now *Siren Land* was begun in May, 1908, *Fountains
in the Sand* was written between December, 1909, and
March, 1910, so the 'good many years' cannot have been
much above four. Well-spent years I should call them.
Douglas was not a fertile writer, and his period of best
production was from *Siren Land* in 1911 to *Alone* in 1921.
There was a revival of production about 1928 to 1931,
but I incline to think this was rather due to anxiety about
some provision for his old age than to a renewal of
inspiration, for these later books are nearly all 'made', and

in some cases are padded by revamping or by reprinting earlier work.

Norman's enthusiasm for Old Calabria had thus persuaded us to make our way to Sicily by land route instead of shipping the car and ourselves direct from Naples to Palermo. It was Pino's subsequent enthusiasm for this trip which persuaded Norman to abandon his dislike for entering my car and join some of our short excursions. One of Pino's favourites was to La Romola (I suppose George Eliot took the name from the village?), but I don't remember that Norman ever came there, and my chief memory of La Romola is of sitting in a large refrigerator, miscalled a *trattoria*, with legs so cold that they were one long ache from toes to knees, and we had to beg for a *scaldino*—a sort of brazier with glowing almond shells— they are ancient, the Romans had them. Meanwhile Pino had been chattering away quite unconscious of any hardship! I do remember that on one excursion with Norman we stood watching some lizards flitting about in the sun, several of them with tiny new-hatched young ones in their mouths. B. was exclaiming over this parental care in reptiles, when Norman interrupted with a sardonic: "Ha! You think they're looking after their offspring? Poof, my dear, they're going to chump them up. Ha!"

He seemed to enjoy these so much that one afternoon, following one of Norman's diatribes against the 'muck' and 'poison' of Florentine restaurants, Pino and I planned to drive him over to Bologna to his favourite 'place' there, dine, and stay the night. This was only half a success. The distance from Florence to Bologna is only a little over a hundred kilometres, but most of the road is over mountains and there are two passes. The weather was bad, and long before we reached the top of the Futa we were in clouds, which cut off all the views of the Apennines we had

promised. The drive naturally took longer than we had
expected. At the restaurant Norman's cook (we found)
had departed, and I think I never had a worse meal in
Bologna la grassa. Finally, Norman and Pino shared a
room, and Norman had a nightmare. In the morning Pino
was quite bitter about it: "All night you make a ghastly
noise as you lament yourself, my dear boy."

Pino told us he was keeping a diary of our Calabria-
Sicily tour, and I believe he did, though I never saw it.
Soon we were told that he intended to use his diaries (I
had seen an earlier one) of his journeys with Norman and
us as a basis for a book. In a letter from Vorarlberg, dated
6 August, 1932, Pino mentions that on rainy days he is
working at "my C.L.S. book"—the C.L.S. being the
burlesque 'Society' to which we were all supposed to
belong. When in 1934 Charles gave me one of the nine
specially printed copies of Pino's *Moving Along* I was a
little puzzled to see that it was dedicated only to Norman
and Charles, and that Charles's inscription (there was
none from Pino) read: "To Richard, fellow-traveller
too." (It is dated 31/5/34.) As I read the book I began
gradually to understand. From Pino's stories I was
familiar with some of the material in the book, and I soon
realised that instead of merely correcting Pino's little
mistakes in grammar and spelling Norman, to save himself
trouble, had re-written the whole book in his own style to
please himself. Thus almost all Pino's special and unique
quality was lost in second-rate Norman Douglas narrative,
with many of his usual clichés—'it stands to reason that',
'what next', 'disheartening' and so forth. Moreover, Pino
had not been allowed to make any but the barest references
to any trips except those taken with Norman, and even
these slight references were treated with not much regard
for fact. Thus, Pino's visit to Tiriolo was with us, and it is

dismissed with the words "I was there with a friend in his car," and the remark that the drive along the mountain-road was 'delicious'. Well, the drive happened to be through clouds and you couldn't see fifty feet in any direction, which adds point to the remark on the next page that from near Tiriolo you can "survey both the Ionian and Tyrrhenian seas", and so you can in fine weather, but Pino didn't see them. Then 'the friend' in the car wanted a drink, and there follows a tale of getting wine from a shop kept by a boy of twelve (of course!), which most certainly didn't happen to us. What did happen is that we went into a little shop to buy postcards, and as I was collecting cards of local costumes I bought that ridiculous one of Calabrian costume reproduced opposite page 128 of *Moving Along*. Pino loved it so much ("*Look* at them! Vot cretins! Vot ——!") that I gave it to him, and Norman cooked up a cock-and-bull story about Pino having received it as a family photograph from the sacristan of the church at Taverna. In a similar light-hearted vein little episodes from Pino's trip with Charles and me are transferred to trips with Norman. One of these refers to a beautiful blue bird with a long black bill which a shepherd boy had caught and was tormenting by letting it flutter with a string tied to its leg. We insisted that Pino should buy it, and he got it for two lire. The bird was taken several miles on in the car and then released. Norman could not have failed to know that this bird episode happened to us, because in Florence I told him about it and tried to describe it. He thought it might have been a roller.

The one occasion in which I am mentioned by name is in connection with an incident which shows me up as an incompetent driver:

"I travelled from Lagonegro with Richard Aldington
and Brigidina in their car" (why no mention of Charles?)
"and we found ourselves snowed up on the heights near
Campo Tenese. We had to telephone Castrovillari for
another car to come up and release us, while we sat
shivering up there in the snow and darkness for long
hours. What a night! I was never more glad to enter
the Hotel d'Atri than at two o'clock next morning."

Well, that's all right, but in fact we did not sit shivering
in cold and darkness until two a.m. We sat for a couple of
hours beside the fire in a road-mender's cottage, and were
eating our dinner in Castrovillari by eight o'clock.
Norman's common sense might have told him that if we
had really been forced to spend eight hours of darkness in
that snow and frost we should all have been ill, if not frost-
bitten.

Having got Pino to his hotel at Castrovillari, Norman
immediately drops our expedition and works up a story of
what happened on another occasion, with great emphasis
on the comic waiter, Moses, so called because of a large
protruding wart on his forehead which was supposed to
make him look like Michelangelo's Moses. In *Moving
Along* we are told that Moses must be spoken to in French,
and a considerable specimen of Moses's discourse in
pidgin French is reproduced—not *very* funny, I think.
Now, of course, Pino had prepared us for Moses and told
us how fond he was of Norman and how warmly he would
greet Pino, and us as Pino's friends. Naturally, I can't
answer for what went on during Pino's visits there with
Norman, but I can swear that not one word of French,
pidgin or otherwise, was spoken to or by Moses in my
hearing, that he disclaimed all knowledge of Il Signor
Douglas, and instead of greeting Pino as an old client

insisted that Pino was our Italian courier, and would not be convinced to the contrary. Pino was furious, and registered himself as *possidente* (capitalist), at which Moses sneered heartily.

There was a sequel to this next morning. We had been given a good enough dinner for Old Calabria, and as usual I had gone off to bed early leaving Pino and Charles to chirrup over their wine. Next morning, just as I was dressed, I heard a timid tap at the door. When I opened it I was staggered to see Pino, shaved, washed and brushed, standing fully clothed except that he had on no trousers and was wearing long under-pants.

"Have you seen my trouser?" he asked anxiously. "Do you know where zhey are?"

"Your trousers! How should I know? Haven't you looked for them?"

"Yes, but I cannot find, I *cannot*. I cannot go in Sicilia without trouser."

At that moment Charles came out of his room, and was put *au courant*.

"Why, don't you remember, Pino," he said gravely, "that last night you were annoyed with Moses for thinking you were a courier? You said that after this you were going to dress like an English gentleman, and that you'd begin by pressing your trousers between your mattresses."

"Did I?" said Pino, "I do not remember vun vurd."

There under Pino's mattress we found his trousers, creased indeed, though not quite as accurately as in Savile Row.

In another book I have told some of Pino's doings in Sicily—how he found a 'deaf-and-dumb' at Castelvetrano, how, learning from Charles that the people of Segesta had sided with the Carthaginians, he 'went against' the Segestans and was disconcerted to find nothing of them

H

remained but a lonely temple, how he became enthusiastic about the tyrant Hieron of Syracuse—or was it
Theron of Akragas?—('a Duce') and was disillusioned,
how he uttered memorable words at the sight of Ragusa,
and how unhappy he was on the evening we spent in a
prim, proper, over-clean north European hotel in
Taormina. Perhaps I did not tell all of these, but there is
one which even if told must be re-told.

I have forgotten in what Sicilian town we were (Pino's
diary if not destroyed might show) when one morning I
went out with him to do the picnic shopping. We carried
with us a wicker flask for wine, and the custom was to
look for 'a lovely vine-shop', where Pino would talk about
coming from Romagna or some such thing, and then ask
for a glass of their best wine. He and Charles would taste
it; if they approved, the flask was filled; if not, they went
and looked for another. This day Pino found a wonderful
place with a row of huge vats behind the counter. While
we were waiting to be attended to we listened to the talk
of two Sicilians beside us. Presently Pino whispered in
my ear: "Have you understood?" "No. Did you?" "Not
vun vurd!" While he was talking to the *padrone* I noticed
the word *gessato* marked on some of the casks, and
presently asked Pino what it meant. "I do not know," he
said vaguely, "I do not sink it mean anything." But I
remembered that *gesso* is the word used for the wet
plaster in ancient fresco painting, and Falstaff's "You
rogue! there's lime in this sack" came into my mind. I
put this tentatively to Pino, and he suddenly became alert.
"My gawd, yes, it means 'chalk'! Vy they must put chalk
in zheir vine?"

I should have let it go at that, but apparently Pino and
Charles whooped up the topic over their wine that night
after we had gone to bed, and decided that we should all

get chalk-stones from gout. Charles, indeed, went so far as to say that he already felt large deposits of chalk in his knees, and proceeded to demonstrate it by writing on the door with them—or so Pino gravely assured me next morning. They had decided, he added, that we must drink no more Sicilian wine, but buy some flasks of Tuscan wine and drink only that for picnic lunch and dinner. I pointed out that this meant driving back to Palermo, the nearest big town where such foreign luxuries as Chianti could be bought; but he insisted, and back we went, loading up with six flasks of two and a half litres. That night we stopped at Cefalù, and, at my suggestion, they put the remaining flasks in my bedroom to avoid the temptation of drinking up our stock too soon. I was just falling asleep when I was startled to see the door open and a stealthy figure enter on tip-toe. I called out sharply to know who it was, and an Italian voice said in a stage whisper: "*Charl!*" At that moment I heard Charles's stifled laughter on the landing—of course, Pino knew that I would forgive Charles what I wouldn't forgive him. I thereupon locked the door, and in the morning found only one of my depot of flasks had disappeared. For some reason we had to be up very early next morning, and I could not help noticing the two robbers were very silent until they urgently approved B.'s suggestion of an early lunch.

A sensation of unappeasable melancholy comes on me when I reflect that almost everything which made the fun and attraction of Pino died with him. We know that men and all they do must perish and, sooner or later, must be wholly forgotten and as if they had never been; but we would rather it was later than sooner, and would fain preserve something of that lost life of those who were our friends. What can I give of Pino but the faintest of dim

portraits, a mere *caput mortuum* of the man? Could
Lawrence have reconstructed him on paper so that at least,
if he could not make us see and experience the living man,
we might hear his voice and glimpse his unconscious
mannerisms? Lawrence did this for others, why not for
Pino, who is unluckily mentioned only in *Pansies* and
casually in the *Letters*? I think Pino escaped record in
Lawrence's novels simply because he did not come really
into Lawrence's life until 1926, although they had met
casually in Cornwall long before; and there was no place
for him in *Lady Chatterley's Lover*. It is absurd of Norman to
assert that Pino was the man who 'knew Lawrence best'.
What of Edward and David Garnett, Middleton Murry,
Aldous Huxley and Martin Secker, not to mention such
friends of Lawrence's younger days as the Chambers,
W. E. Hopkin and A. W. Macleod? And I wonder if Pino
was ever really intimate with Lawrence, whose puritanism
would not have endured Pino's conversations and pranks
when he was 'alluminate' with Chianti. I doubt it. In
spite of his betrayal of Lawrence in his two books (where
the voice and malice are not Pino's but Norman's) I can
testify that around 1930–32 Pino spoke of Lawrence with
the greatest respect for his memory. He even talked of
trying to get permission from the Sindaco of Florence to
put a small memorial tablet on the pine tree near Scandicci
under which Lawrence wrote most of *Lady C*. Would
he have done that if he had felt the dislike and contempt
for Lawrence expressed in his book?

I suppose we must say that Pino was an Italian *im-
provisatore*, in a special style of his own but in the coarse
manner of the old *novellieri*. He put no restraint on the
exuberance of his fancies and language, often encouraged
to go too far by Norman's schoolboy chuckles. Perhaps,
like other artists, Pino might have been improved by a

little restraint. I soon got to know his method of develop-
ing a theme in succeeding versions from its first sketch to
full maturity, and then to decadence. I think the almost
total lack of Pino's characteristic verve and laughter in the
Memoirs versions is due chiefly to Norman's clumsy
handling, but also to the fact that by then Pino was tired of
the old stories. The *Memoirs* version of the tale of the
Bishop of Catania, and of how Pino became his secretary
for a week in London, is pallid indeed compared with
Pino's acted version. I remember but have not the skill to
bring alive again Pino's acting of various scenes, from his
meeting with the sea-sick Bishop on the Channel boat to
the finale of praying together at the Confessor's shrine in
Westminster Abbey—which is the true climax, and
Norman makes the mistake of going on beyond that point.
I should estimate that the telling of the tale at its height of
glory must have occupied close on ten minutes, with Pino
acting first himself, then the Bishop, then himself and the
Bishop in dialogue, with the perfect refrain just at the
right moment: "And always I am the Bishop secretary."
How can one reproduce all that (short of Lawrence's
uncanny memory and genius for writing) in mere words?
In the finale at the shrine Pino gave a stupendous rendering of the lip-movements of this fat old bigot chewing out
his prayers, and Pino obediently imitating him, breaking
off to assure us that only Italians can achieve this impressive appearance of pious devotion because they do not
bother about prayers but simply imagine they are chewing
yards and yards of mounting spaghetti.

I have mentioned how at moments of acute emotion
during dinner (such as Norman's stealing the kidneys)
Pino would rise to his feet, noisily brushing the wine off
his lips with the back of his hand, and denounce with
pointed fore-finger. I wish I could remember his standing

denunciation of James Joyce, which was a most spirited and virulent, though not perhaps very relevant, piece of eloquence. It began, I remember, in Italian. *"Joyce! É un caso di manicomio! Fú nato là,"* pointing, we all instantly knew, to the far distant lunatic asylum of Alphonsine.

An allusion in one of the letters from Pino given here reminds me that, greatly to Norman's displeasure, I had been allowed to read one of Pino's diaries of a trip with Norman. It was written alternately in English and Italian, was quite uninhibited, and contained unsavoury adventures with curly-pated rascals and Greek genii. I have forgotten every word of it except the phrase beyond which I ceased to read. Pino had described (in English) how two young Englishmen with wavy hair had undulated into the hotel where he and Norman were staying, and then breaking into Italian reflected: *"Mi pare un paio di sods."* I thought it only too probable, and closed the book. This diary was unprintable though not unreadable, but it failed to give Pino's real style, which is more apparent in his letters, far as they drop behind his spoken verve. His mistakes, his mispronunciations, his slight mis-spellings contribute toward a special flavour, like that of Rousseau-le-Douanier or some such modern primitive of genius, which was characteristic of Pino's unique manner. Norman was incapable of sympathising with this, even if he had perceived it. Putting on his horn-rimmed classical spectacles Norman ruthlessly turned these Douanier canvases into Alma Tademas. If only he had tried to preserve the naïve and pungent imperfections of Pino's text!

Above all, it seems to me, Norman 'ham'd up' the dialogue of Pino's writings, though he had Pino's voice and manner ever in his ears. Douglas, who genuinely but ignorantly despised Lawrence for his very rare gift of being

able to make the people in his novels each talk with exactly
his own manner and rhythm, had a theory of stylised
dialogue which was fatal to the living word, so that almost
everyone who talks in his books is Douglas-ised into
similarity, a monotony of flippantly doggish worldliness.
Sometimes, he does for a few lines hit the truth of living
speech, as witness this:

". . . at my lowest ebb of vitality, a small carriage
suddenly hove in sight.

" 'How much to Catanzaro?'

"The owner eyed me critically, and then replied in
English:

" 'You can pay twenty dollars.'

"Twenty dollars—a hundred francs! But it is useless
trying to argue with an *americano* (their time is too
valuable).

" 'A dollar a mile?' I protested.

" 'That's so.'

" 'You be damned.'

" 'Same to you, mister,' and he drove off."

That seems to me to have an authenticity which
Norman's dialogue seldom has, except when it is put into
his own person in actuality or in fiction, or into somebody
who may use the same style and mannerisms without too
much awkwardness. That little scrap I have just quoted
seems to me to live. One knows that type of Italian
labourer, who has returned from America filled with self-
conceit because he has been paid far beyond his dreams for
manual labour, and intends to practise what he thinks are
American business methods. Norman has 'got' him in
those few scraps of talk. In that unfortunate failure, *In the
Beginning*, to read which is indeed 'uphill work', there is

not a single character with a touch of personal life, with the striking exception of Fattuta, the old procuress. She sounds as if studied from life.

How far and how disastrously Norman imposed this theory of dialogue may be seen in the following extract from Pino's *Moving Along*. The first speaker is one of the companions of the trip, the second Pino himself:

" 'Have you got your second wind?'
" 'Not yet; I'm still panting.'
" 'Go quite slowly. Get your second wind.'
" 'I think I'll ride. My tongue is dry, and my stomach dreadfully empty after that miserable cup of coffee this morning. I shall get on my mule.'
" 'Nothing of the kind. This excursion has been specially planned to cure your liver trouble. The scrambling is doing you all the good in the world— much better than your pills and consultations and treatments and baths at Montecatini and Chianciano. If you had a walk like this every morning before breakfast for ten years there would be an end to your liver complaints. Now just walk the whole way to the next village, and I'll keep you company.' "

The person who is supposed to be talking to Pino in that bluff and doggish manner is not Norman, but Charles. Charles! Now, of course, nobody can assert that Charles did not say something of the sort, though it sounds so utterly unlike him. He was far more likely to be too sympathetic with Pino's hang-over than to bully him in that Scoto-Teutonic manner. But that last long speech is quite out of character. The tone and manner are all wrong, and nothing like Charles, with his silences, his hesitant manner, his brief sentences. "Nothing of the

kind" is a Norman mannerism, and the whole of the last
two sentences attributed to Charles are Norman Douglas
and nothing but Norman Douglas. (And, by the way, we
are forgetting that this is supposed to be written by Pino.)
Much as I admire Norman as a writer and gladly acknowledge his immense superiority, I don't admire him for
dialogue like that. It is bad art. How many of those over-
worked Norman clichés strangely occur in Pino's pages:
"It stands to reason that . . ." (something absurd which
doesn't stand to reason); "Uphill work!"; "What next!"
and the rest of them. The book itself ends with a device
Norman had not been afraid of repeating, namely a night
walk to and into some Italian village after the electricity
had been switched off. *Moving Along* (a rather Douglas-
like title, by the way) ends up:

"So much I remember distinctly. And also this: that
our way home was all in the dark. The lights of
Genazzano had been extinguished."

Norman was a master of these brief effective endings.
Just look, for instance, at all the skilful endings to chapter
after chapter in *Old Calabria*. If they were not so grace-
fully done, you might call them a formula.

5

MENTION of that excursion to Bologna with Pinorman
has reminded me of the last I ever took with them
both. Early in 1937 I was in Florence for a short time,
and one evening Pino said that Norman was tired of being
shut up all winter in Florence and wanted to run over to
Lucca for lunch. Of course I said I would take them—
and Norman arrived at the rendezvous bringing with him
(uninvited) a depraved-looking slum child whose behaviour
during the day left absolutely no doubt as to the nature of
their relationship. There were two things about this
piece of insolence which annoyed me. In the first place,
although I had never presumed to criticise him, I had
always kept wholly aloof from these conquests of his; and
in the second place it was a blatant example of his habit of
exploiting his friends while professing the noble sentiments
I have quoted from *Looking Back*. The moment I saw this
'pestilential' young companion I knew that Pino had been
set on to suggest the trip merely for the purpose of
providing the creature with a free joy-ride in an American
car. I think if I had known as much then as I now know I
should have refused to take them. I wish I had.

Norman was unscrupulous about involving other people
in these strange amours which from a legal point of view
were criminal, and resulted from time to time in his being
'considerably fussed' by the attentions of the police—so
much so that during the 1930s he had to fly from Austria to

Italy leaving all his baggage behind, and from Italy to France. He had eagerly grasped at the offer of two guileless young Americans I knew later in Paris to lend him their flat "so he could meet a young friend of his." They, of course, had no idea of what they were doing, but Norman knew perfectly well that if the situation had been discovered they would have been in serious legal trouble. He also risked Pino's liberty. One day in Florence I found Pino in a great rage. The evening before, he told me, he had come by sheer accident on a guttersnipe on the stairs of the apartment house where both Norman and Pino had flats. Pino discovered that this boy was about to call on Norman, with instructions to say if questioned that he was taking a parcel to Signor Orioli. He was indeed carrying a brown paper parcel addressed to Pino in Norman's hand and containing a lot of old newspapers. Pino was really angry about this, and declared he would not talk with Norman again. It may have been on this occasion that Pino stuffed a sock or something into the private speaking-tube between his flat and Norman's. But, of course, Pino was far too weak-willed to resist Norman, and in three or four days they were going about together as usual, though not, I think, quite on the old footing.

I thought I had given an account of Pino's prosecution in Florence for publishing an indecent book, but as I cannot find any mention of it in the place I expected to find it, the story must be lost in some periodical. There is a partially true account in Pinorman's *Memoirs of a Bookseller*, but not the whole story. Under the title of *The Last of the Medici*, Pino had published an English translation by Harold Acton of an eighteenth-century Italian pamphlet on Gian Gastone, the last Medici Grand Duke, with an introduction by Norman. Though it was badly written and rather scurrilous this pamphlet was a historical curiosity, having on a much lower scale the sort of interest which hangs about Suetonius. Just as his lives of the Cæsars were written to disparage the extinct dynasty and reconcile the Romans to the new one, so this Gian Gastone pamphlet was written to vilify the last Medici and persuade the Florentines that the new Austrian Grand Duke was a liberator. In the course of the narrative Gian Gastone was accused of various sexual excesses and abnormalities. According to Pino, at the last moment before the book went to press, Norman, jolly with the wine flask, amused himself by inserting in the text certain of the 'unprintable' English words. What Norman didn't realise was that some international arrangement had been made whereby various countries undertook to prosecute the publishers of 'obscene literature' in English within their territories. And though ostensibly directed against the merely vulgar behind-the-counter stuff this legislation was really aimed at the printers and publishers of such writers as James Joyce, D. H. Lawrence and Norman himself—that book of Limericks of his very nearly involved Lytton Strachey in serious trouble.

Anyway, if Norman did insert any of these fetish-laden words in someone else's translation it was a foolish and unscrupulous thing to do. A copy of the book had been found in the English mails, and Pino and the authors were being prosecuted; but Acton had left for China before this storm arose, and Norman had 'evaporated' at the first hint of trouble. All this came out over dinner at Fusi's the night before the second hearing of Pino's case, when the poor little man at last confessed what was making him so gloomy and troubled. Apparently Norman had told him (for what reason, I can't conceive) that I was not to know about it.

Next day I went along to the Court with Pino, and—for

what it was worth—offered to give my evidence as a
reviewer of the book in a respectable English newspaper.
In an English Court the case would have been pre-
judged before it was ever heard, the defence would have
been contemptuously swept aside, and Pino heavily fined
or imprisoned. The defence of Pino's counsel was that the
book complained of was a translation of a book which
circulated freely in Italy, so where was the breach of
Italian law? The prosecution said the translation was not
exact, and the magistrate had ordered a remand while text
and translation were reported on by a professor or professors of the University. As far as I remember, the
professors reported that the translation was of high literary
quality and exact 'except for a few words'. They did not
specify which words, the prosecution did not press the
point, and the magistrate ignored an attempt to prejudice
the case by dragging in the irrelevant issue of *Lady
Chatterley's Lover*. Pino and the printer were acquitted. I
think that, apart from the fairness of the Court, Pino
owed something to his appearance in the dock. He had
put on his best clothes, was well groomed, and somehow
seemed to look so innocent you could not believe any ill of
such a good man. St. Agnes herself could not have looked
more innocent, and then with what politeness and in
what 'educated' Italian he gave his evidence! Pino
attached too much importance to this accompanying him
to Court, for I was in no way involved and ran no risk
whatever. It was a day lost, perhaps, though, like Pino, I
had been amused by some of the preceding cases; and had
learned to respect the humanity of the Italian Court. I find
an echo of this in Pino's *Memoirs*, where I am over-praised
for something I wrote about the case in a newspaper, but
nothing is said of my being with Pino in Court. That
might have suggested the question: Why wasn't his

closest friend, Norman Douglas, there too?

These are aspects of Norman's life and character which that future biographer will have to deal with and to explain. The tendency of modern political and social life is all toward relieving men of responsibility for their individual lives while compelling them to make all conceivable sacrifices for the benefit of an abstract and mythical 'State'—it is in fact the revival of slavery in the name of popular democracy for the benefit of the State's exploiters. Something of the same process has taken place in some schools of moralists—the tendency is to relieve the 'patient' (no longer a sinner) from responsibility for his impulses and consequent actions. Homosexuals are explained as the result of some psychological influence in childhood (in the case of men, a doting and too much adored mother) or some physical imbalance of hormones. No doubt there is something in all this, but at the risk of sounding out-of-date I must record my conviction that in Norman's case these deviations were not the result of psycho-physical misfortunes but simply due to what old-fashioned people called 'vice'. He was looking for new sensations, and an experiment became a habit. Apparently, he was able to experiment with opium and hashish, and then cut free.

Readers of *Looking Back* will remember that on page 240 he diverges from the story of Anyuta and Helen (which last I have completed earlier in this book from my recollections of Norman's telling of the tale) to follow up the re-collections suggested by Anyuta's malacca cane. This takes his memory into the back streets of Naples in 1897 (when he was twenty-eight) to make one of his unpleasant bargains with a mother for her young daughter. On his way back from this interview, Norman was suddenly attacked, hit on the head by the girl's younger brother, and

half-stunned. Norman complained of this to the boy's
mother and she made him kneel down and beg the gentleman's pardon for having attacked him. "He was like his
sister, and even prettier," says Norman meaningly, and
later on says:

". . . not long afterwards the boy fell in love with
me desperately, as only a southern boy of his age can do;
so blindly that at a hint from myself he would have
abandoned his work and family and everything else."

Norman then goes on to state (what some people may
have difficulty in believing) that the boy's mother and sister
thought "that it was the most natural thing in the world"
and congratulated Norman on having "waked the boy up"!
From this episode he dated the switch-over of his erotic
impulses from women to boys, and I have already mentioned his quotation of the Rufinus epigram and Norman's
opinion that the reverse was almost impossible. Anyway,
I should say that story shows that the change had nothing
to do with any innate predisposing causes but was under-
taken merely out of curiosity—vice. It might be urged
with some show of reason that the word 'vice' carries a
moral reprobation and implies doing something a man
believes to be wrong for the sake of vanity or pleasure, and
that, since Norman did not recognise any moral standards
(but only an adjustable æsthetic standard) he cannot justly
be accused of 'vice'. It is a specious argument, and can be
met from his own writings. In one of his 'knock-'em-
flat' dogmatisings about a boys' school in Calabria he says
emphatically that "the immature stage of development, far
from being artificially shortened, should be prolonged by
every possible means." I don't believe it, but never mind
—nothing could be so effective in 'artificially shortening'

the 'immature stage' in boys as the tamperings with them
of Norman Douglas.

Just as the written version of the tale of Helen is
inferior to the story as Norman told it by word of mouth,
so it was with this story of Naples and its slum-dwellers.
In the *Looking Back* version no motive is given for the boy's
attack except that his sister had said he was a "hot-
tempered and reckless young devil" (she had soon picked
up Norman's phraseology!) and that "something awful will
happen if he finds out about us". In the version told over
the dinner-table a much more dramatic motive was given
for the boy's attack, namely, that he was already in love
with Norman and tried to kill him, not "to avenge his
sister's honour", but because he was jealous of her. In this
version nothing was said about the sister's prophetic words
of warning, and Norman described the attack as a complete
surprise. It was the shock of that surprise which led
Norman to investigate these pseudo-Hellenic by-ways of
desire. Possibly the printed version is the more accurate,
but the version told is not only more dramatic but more
plausible. Why did the boy make the attack if he was not
already jealous? The story certainly seems better motivated
in the spoken than in the *Looking Back* version.

That biographer will have to put in some 'uphill work'
trying to explain on psychological grounds how a man in
many ways so distinguished, in appearance so dignified,
with accomplishments and all kinds of out-of-the-way
learning seldom brought together in one mind, cultivated a
vice which seems so odious and degrading. It is true that
the two or three specimens of Norman's conquests I
happened to see were peculiarly detestable-looking
children, but that may not have been their fault, though I
must protest that I never saw creatures less like the 'Greek
genii', 'pretty boys' and 'curly-pated rascals' who are

always being hinted about in Norman's writings. Indeed,
I am convinced that for those whose tastes leave them
completely inactive in these pursuits they are less repulsive in literature than in life. The Greeks! We read of
Harmodius and Aristogeiton "who struck the tyrant down"
in Athens. "Noble-hearted sods!" we exclaim, though
historically it appears that they bungled the affair, getting
only the less dangerous of their two men, and losing their
own lives. But this is still the heroical epoch of 'Greek
love' and Norman's tastes belong to the later epochs of the
Anthology on the Anacreontea. No doubt it was sheer
romanticism on my part, but when I used to read those
beautifully formed little poems to Bathyllus and Demo-
philus and Myiscus and Plato's enthusiastic praises of
Charmides and Lysis and Phædrus, I never for a moment
imagined them as guttersnipes from the back streets of
Naples, Florence and London. The sterner moralist will
no doubt ask what difference that made to the moral
turpitude involved. To which I can only plead that from
the point of view of æsthetics there is all the difference in
the world between an aristocratic *kalokagathos* beside the
Ilissus and a cockney street arab.

It would be strange if a man so realistic and practical as
Norman should have beheld these unsavoury creatures
through the golden mist of Hellenic ideals. Was there
indeed any place for ideals in the philosophy of this
antinomian hedonist? He was no modest follower of
Epicurus, practising frugality as pleasure. I should say he
went far beyond Aristippus in praising purely sensual
pleasure without the restraint of any moral law, the very
existence of which Norman denied. He preached, and
presumably practised, a doctrine which does not seem easily
distinguishable from selfishness and 'm'en-fous-tism'. In
quoting earlier in this book his letter of the 27th

September, 1931, I left out a few lines, but it seems to me that in the interest of truth they should be quoted and that their place is here:

> "Fact is, I never write nowadays unless I want somebody to do something for me—sad, but true. And I can't think of anything you can do for me even now . . ."

No doubt that was meant to be sardonic humour, but it is undeniably close to the bald truth. The experience of others with Norman may have been different—I hope it was and that they will put it on record—but in all the time I was with him I seldom saw him put himself out in the least or do anything much for another person. I still clearly remember my astonishment at a little episode which happened early in our acquaintance. We were walking together on the Lungarno when we passed a wild-looking, ragged, haggard fellow. "Look at him," said Norman, "you can see he's starving," and left it to me to turn back, ask the man if he was hungry and give him some money, while Norman merely made some slighting remark when I rejoined him, and continued his conversation. This may have been reaction from over-generosity in youth; and then he had learned in the harsh school of privation to keep his purse tight-shut. Or was it self-protection against something ugly and distressing? Lawrence told his American friend, Brewster, that Norman had entirely dropped Frieda and himself during their war days of poverty and persecution, on purely hedonistic grounds of self-protection. It may be so, but I think Lawrence did not ever know the persecution and hardship which Norman himself suffered during the war. Again, I have heard it said that, although Norman was in

Lisbon at the time, this hedonistic self-protection kept him from ever going to see his best friend, Pino, when he was dying in Lisbon during the war; but I don't even know that the facts are as reported, and prefer to think the tale a calumny.

In any case he did recommend and, within my experience, did practise this callous self-protection. It is no doubt my misfortune in failing to win Norman's regard which led him to write the cynicism I have just quoted from his letter. He had an ungracious manner at times, which seemed strange in so well-bred a man who was so disgusted with Lawrence for not being a gentleman. At his request, I sent or brought him snuff and English pipe tobacco, and bundles of fifty Toscano cigars from other parts of Italy where he thought them better than in Florence—and of course I considered this an honour. But . . . well, during a difficult crisis in my life I wrote him from France a (doubtless too lengthy) letter, and said I thought of coming to Florence to be near him and Pino, and get his (Norman's) advice. A few lines of friendly sympathy were doubtless what I was fishing for, but the letter I got brushed off my difficulties in half a sentence and the rest of it was devoted to precise instructions about the pound of English tobacco I was to bring him. He got his tobacco. At another time he came to spend a few days with me in a little cottage I rented on the Côte des Maures. By this time I had learned, or thought I had learned, that he disliked what I might call 'upper class' French cooking and believed (most erroneously) that all vintage wines sold on the Riviera were 'muck'. It was his taste which was at fault. At any rate, wishing to please him, I arranged with my cook (an excellent peasant cook) to serve us only Provençal dishes—such as *bouillabaisse*, *aioli*, and, of course, his roast lamb with the kidneys—and got in bonbons of good white and red *vin ordinaire* from Gassin, which is about the best in the district. The only comment he made was on a dish of fresh young peas (and not those giant marrowfats of which he has complained so eloquently) which in accordance with French habit was sent to table with a pat of fresh butter on them. He said what a pity they were 'swimming in grease'! No doubt they should have been swimming in water and covered with chives in the high German fashion. At the end of his stay he suggested a drive to the café at Bormes, and when I asked what he would drink, Norman said: "You sit still. I'll go and see what they've got." He came back with two bottles of vintage champagne and ham sandwiches. This was handsome enough, but from his manner and a sneer or two I took it to be a satirical comment on my uncouth hospitality—in deference to his alleged dislike for vintage wine I had been giving him Ackerman instead of champagne. Was I over-sensitive? I would merely say that I have entertained other guests, including Charles and Frere—who had better opportunities than Norman of knowing the best—and *always* had the feeling they knew I had done my best to please them. Doubtless they could have done themselves much better at the Savoy or La Pérouse, but they never allowed me to feel so.

At that time I did not realise how highly Norman esteemed his own writings and how contemptuous he was of his contemporaries, though I had noticed he seldom praised any living author. A man who writes with so much complacency to tell us just how and where he wrote his books, and how critics failed to understand the novels he wrote which few people read, and at the same time dismisses both Dickens and Flaubert as unimportant—well, such a man has a good conceit of himself as an author. Let us admit frankly that nearly all authors over-estimate the value of their works, but I think this attitude of 'Me first and the rest nowhere' is characteristic rather of the amateur, the *demi-raté*, the highbrow who is so afraid you will see how much he yearns for something more substantial that a refined *succès d'estime*, than of the professional author who has to sink or swim in the stream and knows that the stream carries 99.9 per cent of all new books to oblivion in at most thirty years. I remember this being put to me by a very successful though not illiterate professional writer. It was just after demobilisation in 1919 and we had been guests at a dinner of a literary sort in Arlington Street. We left together and went down Piccadilly, enjoying the sensation of being in evening dress (at least I did by sheer contrast), and I said to him that during the war years I had almost determined to give up any thought of a literary career since I had come to realise that my slender talent could not possibly rival even the tenth-rate authors of the past. He took me up on this, saying: "That's the attitude of the amateur, who ignores his contemporaries and over-estimates himself by comparing himself only with the academically acceptable authors. We can't rival them, because they came before us, and if we accept their standards the best we can do is to be their imitators. But we can say something to our contemporaries of life as it is now, which Homer and Shakespeare never dreamed of—no, and not even our friend Wells! Maybe we're not much good. So what? Let's do our best and go out of business when we stop selling. Do you *want* to be praised in the little highbrow reviews? Let me warn you that lack of success is the *sine qua non* of that parochial fame."

Salutary words to a young highbrow! And I wish now that I had taken them more seriously, though I hope they did save me from the worst. Now, Norman was saved

from the parochialism of literary cliques simply because
as a young man he never got into one, but I think in later
days he had some of the airs of the highly superior person
whose books come out in an edition of 500 copies, 'of
which' 100 are signed by the author. But what particularly interests me about that little discourse now is the
courtesy with which that highly successful writer included
in his own literary class a quite unknown beginner who
had made a false start, whereas Norman was always careful,
by reticences and covert sneers, to mark his superiority.

6

INEVITABLY any discussion or reminiscence of Norman Douglas must include *South Wind*. Whether you are considering his personality or those views and prejudices about life and things we call his 'philosophy' or his greatness as a writer, you have to take in *South Wind*. If it is true that every authentic and superior writer produces one work which stands above the others and symbolises him to a world which has no time to read, then Douglas certainly achieved it with this book. This is the work which made his reputation and by which he is known. Though it stands related on one side to the Italian travel books, and on the other to *How About Europe?*, it is above and apart from them, and has less in common with his other attempts at writing. It was different from his other more abstruse books, where the problem was to work off a few hundred copies on more or less wealthy *dilettanti* at as high a price as possible. Coming out in a dismal war period, with its author in poverty-stricken exile, without any of the careful pre-publication advertising of cliques and coteries, purely on its merits, *South Wind* succeeded— and not merely as a *succès d'estime*. In the first thirty years of its life *South Wind* went through twenty-one impressions in England, from which I infer that it had a sturdy unkillable growth as an essential book. The conception of the book was original, and its freshness, vigour and wit evidently recommended it to many readers.

That being so, it seems strange that Norman is comparatively little known outside the English-speaking countries. One would suppose that a writer so cosmopolitan would be widely known and translated on the Continent, but this does not appear to be the case. At the time of writing, Cecil Woolf's bibliography has not been published, but the list I have seen includes only six translations for all Europe. Yet Lawrence in translations may be counted by dozens, and Italy is even bringing out his voluminous works complete; and that in spite of Norman's continuous efforts to discredit Lawrence both as a writer and a person. Perhaps Continental readers enjoy just those English characteristics which Norman never had, and Lawrence, in spite of his cosmopolitan wanderings, never lost.

Of course, there is not much reliance to be placed on the judgments of a 'literary Paris', which is extremely self-centred and not well acquainted with foreign literatures and languages. Even the 'informed opinion' of specialists is too often a slavish repetition of the views which were current when they spent a year in an English University. The fallacious twitterings of some lecturing prig of fifteen years ago may regrettably still be heard echoing in this week's or month's 'latest news' of English literature in Paris.

This does not in the least apply to my friend, J. S., who has written successful plays and novels in his own language, and yet knows our literature as very few Englishmen know French literature; and I accidentally discovered recently that he had made a close study of Norman Douglas. How well J. S. knows English may be judged from the fact that when long ago I was introduced to him in Paris, I spent a whole evening in his company without even suspecting that he was not English, so

perfectly did he speak the language even to its finest
shades. In spite of which he remains very much a Parisian
in his literary judgments, and though I totally disagree
with his views I have thought readers might be interested
to hear them (as well as I can recollect), from a conversation we had when I had begun work on this book.
J. S., motoring to Spain, dropped in to see me, found me
at a table covered with books and old letters and asked:
"What now?" I told him—a holiday book, at any rate a
very informal little book of personal recollections and
notes on Norman, Pino and Charles Prentice, their
publisher, merely with the idea of giving some first-hand
details to future biographers of Douglas. I added that
even if they proved worthless for such a purpose, they
might interest a few of Pinorman's friends and introduce
them to others who had not known them. J. S. then
asked where I had got to, and I confessed that on his
arrival I was facing two dreary thoughts. The first was that
in trying to give only authentic personal memories I had
been somehow led to say too much of me—I like a book to
have no 'I' in it. The second was that I had reached the
pompous conclusion that Norman was an 'antinomian
hedonist' (which might be better said in English as a
'lawless pleasure-seeker'), and was wondering if I ought to
try to prove it from the pages of *South Wind*.

"*South Wind*," said J. S., picking up one of the different
editions lying on the table, "I remember they seemed
delighted with it at our Embassy in London."

"I didn't know you'd been in the French diplomatic?"

"Oh, yes, but like Douglas I soon resigned, though not
for the same reasons. Our Ambassador at the time was
enchanted with *South Wind*, and made us all read it. He
said it was *une œuvre magistrale* and thought it proved something—I forget what."

"You admired it, of course?"

"Well, yes, at first. I was young and knew nothing of literature. Later I saw it was really one more *roman à tiroirs* . . ."

"My dear friend!" I protested. "Surely not. You are abusing language."

"How else would you define that Highland cairn of unrelated episodes, that Naples aquarium tank of undeveloped characters related only by propinquity . . .?"

"A great book in the tradition of Peacock," I urged.

"Peacock? Ah yes, a gifted *littérateur*, but not a novelist; a producer of conversation pieces, shall we say, like those weird nineteenth-century 'painters' of yours. A novel is not a series of conversations any more than a picture is a moment in the fifth act of a play. A novel is character in action."

"Then you don't allow ideas in a novel?"

"How can you have a novel without them? But they must always be strictly relevant to the action, not introduced merely to fill up space when the author's invention flags. More than half *South Wind* is padding, witty and amusing no doubt, but still padding, and a significant first indication that the author here did not understand his craft. What is the theme of *South Wind*? The dissolvent action of a southern climate and people on a puritan British temperament as typified by the Colonial Bishop, Heard, who is thus led to condone a planned murder. Ingenious but over-done; in any case a theme for a closely-constructed short story. Here it is intolerably padded and prolonged by mere talk and the author's discourses on such not wholly relevant topics as Monsignor Perelli, the Little White Cows, the fountains of Nepenthe, Saint Eulalia, and so forth—to which I would add the ramblings of those garrulous old bores, Caloveglia and Keith. What

after all is the 'philosophy' of *South Wind* to which you
have given such a portentous pseudo-Greek name? What
is the view of life brought us by this rickety 'vehicle'?
Simply the Burlington Bertie Byronism of such gentlemanly and *démodés* parasites as George Moore and Oscar
Wilde . . ."

"Forgive me if I interrupt you," I said indignantly. "I
never heard anyone compare Douglas and George Moore,
and the view that Norman had anything in common—as a
literary artist—with Oscar Wilde has been amply refuted
by Mr. Willie King."

"Who is Mr. Willie King?"

"At one time Douglas evidently intended to appoint
him literary executor, for in that character Mr. King
wrote an introduction to the 1946 re-edition of *South
Wind*. But he changed his mind and appointed Mr.
Kenneth Macpherson. In any case Mr. King rates as one of
our most subtle æsthetes, and is probably our greatest
living authority on . . ."

"On?"

"On . . ."

And here, at the risk of intruding once more that *moi
haïssible*, I have to admit that I should never allow myself
to get drawn into discussions like this. When someone I
like, as I like J. S., unexpectedly attacks a writer who has
meant so much to me, I grow flurried, defend clumsily,
forget things, and in short display all the symptoms
of *l'esprit au bas de l'escalier*. I could not remember
Mr. King's authoritative studies, and I had later to
ask a friend. . . . Keramics. Of course, keramics!
And Sarah, Duchess of Marlborough. . . . Indispensable
topics.

To cover my confusion I turned up Mr. King's brilliant
and authorised *Introductory Letter* to the 1946 *South Wind*,

and pointed out that he there says that nobody today gives "more than half a second" to Oscar Wilde, adding that Wilde's 'nonsense' has nothing whatever in common with *South Wind*. "So, you see, you are wrong."

J. S. laughed and said: "Curious, I know the English publisher of the most recent selection of Wilde's work, and he told me nearly 25,000 copies had been taken by the public. I expect Mr. King meant by 'nobody' that he and his friends haven't read Wilde, who said: 'Nothing is so dangerous as being too modern; one is apt to grow old-fashioned quite suddenly.' Anyone who has read Wilde and Douglas can see there is something in common between the hedonisms of the two authors. In England I should say it stems from Pater, who picked it up from Gautier and ultimately Goethe—at each stage of borrowing there was a decline. In the end it became a form of Second Empire class-insolence, so faithfully echoed by George Moore in *Memoirs of My Dead Life* and *Confessions of a Young Man*. Douglas is the last of all these, for much of his seeming originality is due to the fact that he was so belated. He had little or no touch with the literary and intellectual life of his time, and when by accident he had he didn't like it. The first writers he came to know were Conan Doyle and Marion Crawford. He was over forty when through Ford Madox Hueffer he met Conrad and Hudson."

"What on earth does that matter?" I protested. "A writer is to be judged by the quality of his writings, not by the reputation of his literary friends. Some of the finest writers—Hudson and Conrad among them—have been aloof and solitary, like Norman himself, most fortunately outside the little literary swim."

"Agreed, agreed." And for once I felt I had scored off J. S., because, being Paris-and-London and *à la mode*, he is

rather apt to take to himself and friends the Miltonic:
"Not to know me argues yourself unknown". "I was only
trying to point out," he went on, "that by starting a quarter
of a century or more behind the times Douglas seemed
new to an ignorant generation when the wheel of literary
fashion once more brought into temporary favour the
gentleman of wit and fashion about town."

"Now, really! A man who spent years of his life out of
great cities and cared nothing for literary modes . . ."

"Certainly, he did it with a difference . . ."

"Which is what counts . . ." I put in.

"He had his scientific interests of the early Darwinian
epoch, his antiquarianism which to me suggests the hobby-
horse of an auld Dominie, his walks and mountaineering,
his Austrian and Calabrian peasants, his diplomatic experiences in Russia. He added a Teutonic truculence to
the more timid and urban hedonism of the two Anglo-
Irishmen. He had a real or affected indifference to the
value of human life—other people's lives. He had read
Nietzsche . . ."

"What hadn't he read?"

"A good deal, I should say. In *Late Harvest* he reprints an
article of forty years earlier in which he cites Pasteur as an
example of the modern atheistic scientist who has no time
for 'a fixed ritual of worship' and asks why Pasteur should
worship and whom. Now if there is one fact known to all
the world except this bigoted Scot atheist it is that Pasteur
was a devout Catholic . . ."

"Well," I said, after verifying the passage J. S. pointed
out, "let him among us writers who has never pulled a
boner make the first jeer."

He returned to the copy of *South Wind* and began turning
the pages.

"I don't know why you are so cowed by the opinion of

Mr. Willie King," he said, "but I think I can prove out of his own book that Douglas copied the style or turn of the Oscar Wilde 'epigram' or 'paradox', just as he quotes Wyndham Lewis without acknowledgment or quotation marks."

"*What!*" I exclaimed incredulously.

"Half a minute—wait—yes! here it is—'Ships tossing at sea; minds firmly anchored to the commonplace'. Straight out of Lewis's 1914 *Blast Manifesto*."

"Good God, so it is. Do you know, I've read *South Wind* a dozen times and never noticed that!"

"I expect Douglas thought it would never be noticed. In 1917 Lewis was considered a wild man, and anyway he was on the Western Front as a bombardier."

"Does he take direct from Wilde too?"

"Oh no. His Wildeisms are 'in the manner of'. Let me find you some. How about this: 'Animals also have their sufferings, but they are not encouraged to tell us about them. Perhaps that is why God made them dumb'."

"Well, yes, in a way it is Wilde, but, as Sancho Panza told the world, one swallow doesn't make a spring."

"How many imitation Oscar swallows from *South Wind* do you want? Two? 'There is so much goodness in real life. Do let us keep it out of our books.' Three? 'To want a wife, Duchess, is better than to need one. Especially if it happens to be our neighbour's.' Four? 'Is it true that you used to say, in your London days, that no season was complete without a ruined home?' Five? 'When people cease to reflect they become idealists.' Six? 'I find everything useful and nothing indispensable. I find everything wonderful and nothing miraculous.' Seven? 'You are thinking of your own mother. You forget that you never see her. Any son can live with any mother under those circumstances.' Eight? 'Nothing ages a man like living always with the same woman.' Nine? 'Altogether the question that confronts me is not whether morality is worth talking about, but whether it's worth laughing at.' Ten? 'To feel self-righteous, or to feel sinful, is quite an innocent form of self-indulgence'."

"All right," I said, "I'm counted out. Now how about proving that La Rochefoucauld was an imitator of Wilde? You invented some of those."

"How well you know your author—nearly as well as Mr. King. I'll show you the texts."

I took the book and had to confess he had quoted exactly and fairly.

"So much for Douglas and Wilde," said J. S. "Now, have you a copy of Moore's *Confessions* here?"

"I think so."

"Thanks. Ah, yes, here we are. Please note that what I am going to read you was published in 1886 when Douglas was still a schoolboy:

" 'Nature provided me with as perfect a digestive apparatus, mental and physical, as she ever turned out of her workshop; my stomach and brain are set in the most perfect equipoise possible to conceive, and up and down they went and still go on with measured movement, absorbing and assimilating all that is poured into them without friction or stoppage. This book is a record of my mental disgestions; but it would take another series of confessions to tell of the dinners I have eaten, the champagne I have drunk! and the suppers! seven dozen of oysters, pâté de foie gras, heaps of truffles, salad, and then a walk home in the early morning, a few philosophical reflections suggested by the appearance of a belated street-sweeper, then sleep, quiet and gentle sleep.

" 'I have had the rarest, the finest friends. I have loved my friends; the rarest wits of my generation were my boon companions; everything conspired to enable me to gratify my body and my brain; and do you think this would have been so if I had been a good man? If you do you are a fool, good intentions and bad greed go to the wall, but subtle selfishness with a dash of unscrupulousness pulls more plums out of life's pie than the seven deadly virtues. If you are a good man you want a bad man to convert. If you are a bad man you want a bad one to go on the spree with.' "

"Now from what I've read and been told of him Norman Douglas does not seem to have been nearly as successful as Moore claims to have been, though perhaps at thirty-five he was. But at any rate you can see from that passage how closely Douglas's 'philosophy of life' was derived from George Moore. . . . Half a minute—here's another one which Douglas has plagiarised shamelessly time and again:

" 'All men of inferior genius, Victor Hugo and Mr. Gladstone, take refuge in humanitarianism. Humanitarianism is a pigsty, where liars, hypocrites, and the obscene in spirit congregate; it has been since the great Jew conceived it, and it will be so till the end. Far better the blithe modern pagan in his white tie and evening clothes, and his facile philosophy.' "

"Well," I said, "there are moods in which I am inclined to agree with much of that."

"As you please," he said, "but don't forget you would be agreeing with Moore, not with Douglas. And as to Wilde and the lack of effect his alleged 'nonsense' is said to have had on Douglas—give me your copy of *Dorian Gray*—yes, here it is:

" 'Don't squander the gold of your days, listening to
the tedious, trying to improve the hopeless failure, or
giving away your life to the ignorant, the common and
the vulgar. These are the sickly aims, the false ideals of
our age. Live! Live the wonderful life that is in you!
Let nothing be lost upon you. Be always searching for
new sensations. Be afraid of nothing. A new Hedonism
—that is what our century wants.'

"That is Wilde in 1890. My dear fellow, your Norman
Douglas whom you think so wonderful and admire so much
is old hat, and was the day he was published. The
illiteracy of the age made his success, for most people in
England were already ignorant of his predecessors.
Norman Douglas is George Moore's chappie of the 1880s,
with a German gymnasium education, hob-nail boots and a
taste for inferior wines. He has a lizard in his Scotch
bonnet, specimens of feldspar in one pocket and Baedeker's
Guide to Southern Italy in the other. His path is strewn
with broken boys and empty bottles and his eyelids are a
little bleary . . ."

And here this phase of our discussion came abruptly to
an end, for I was so much annoyed by this unfairness and
disrespect to Norman and his work that we came near to
the first real quarrel in a long friendship; but drew back
just in time. We passed on eventually to a discussion of
novel-writing in general, and J. S. made some further
comments on *South Wind* which I shall try to summarise a
little later in this chapter. Meanwhile, after his departure,
I had to admit to myself that J. S. had to some extent made
good his contention that Norman's 'philosophy of life'
owed much to Moore and Wilde, and that it is ridiculous
to deny the influence of Wilde on *South Wind*. Indeed I
then recollected that long ago when in Norman's presence

I had once deplored the 'greenery-yallery' tendency of
Wilde's earlier writings, but Norman wouldn't allow it.
"Wilde's work is a yea-saying to life," he said.

J. S. then took up the point that Wilde and Norman
had in common the habit of boasting of themselves as
'gentlemen', though as a matter of fact both were professional writers. The position of 'gentleman', J. S. maintained, was evidently looked upon as a pre-requisite for
doing and getting what one wanted at other peoples'
expense. Mr. George Moore of Moore Park was another
of these 'gentlemen', and strangely enough not one of the
three was an Englishman. In England, he thought, even in
the nineteenth-century the conception of 'gentleman' still
carried with it some faint aura of *noblesse oblige*—
though under pressure from me J. S. was forced to admit
that this had been largely the work of a vulgar Jew
adventurer called Disraeli. I also reminded him that the
'antinomian hedonist' traits of our Scoto-Irish trio had
been hit off long before by Arthur Hugh Clough in a
poem which is too often overlooked:

"They may talk as they please about what they call pelf,
And how one ought never to think of one's-self,
How pleasures of thought surpass eating and drinking,
My pleasure of thought is the pleasure of thinking
How pleasant it is to have money, heigh-ho!
How pleasant it is to have money . . .

One ought to to be grateful, I quite apprehend,
Having dinner and supper and plenty to spend,
And so suppose now, while the things go away,
By way of a grace we all stand up and say
How pleasant it is to have money, heigh-ho!
How pleasant it is to have money . . .

I ride, and I drive, and I care not a damn,
The people look up and they ask who I am;
And if I should chance to run over a cad,
I can pay for the damage, if ever so bad.
So useful it is to have money, heigh-ho!
So useful it is to have money!"

Having made a note of the poem—for needless to say, a
critic does not waste time looking for poetry—J. S. went
on to point out that, with the possible exception of Wilde
as lecturer and reviewer, none of the three did any urgent
work or knew the threat of want until well over thirty.
He thought that this long irresponsible boyhood might
account for the equally long immaturity of both Moore
and Douglas as writers. They both became real writers
instead of *dilettanti* under the pressure of needing money.
Yet they clung to a fictional status of 'gentlemen', as if an
unearned income is the first condition of genius.

"How would you define *The Importance of Being Earnest?*"
J. S. asked, and, without waiting for an answer he obviously
did not want, said: "It is an amoral social farce of satiric
intent which through laughter mocks Victorian Society, its
pretentions and prejudices and humbugs. *South Wind* is an
amoral intellectual farce of satiric intent which sets out to
destroy the humanitarian culture and conventional morals
which had survived from that period into Edwardian days,
for the people in *South Wind* are all Edwardian." Both play
and novel, J. S. thought, should now be read as period
pieces, for you can no more discover the idle opulence of
John Worthing in an Albany turned into an *ergastulum* of
laborious hacks remotely connected with literature than
you can find Caloveglia, Keith, Van Koppen and peace on
an over-crowded Capri seething with tourists. "But," I
protested, "unless we are to read nothing but newspapers,

American propaganda and Blue Books (which indeed may soon be made compulsory reading for all while the British Museum Library burns) we have nothing to read but period pieces. Everything written pre-1940 is now 'period', especially those London School of Economics 'scientific working plans for the future' which were to bring us such peace, such plenty, such glory and such happiness. Remember the 'agrobiologists', whose one fear was a fearful glut of foods? The only way to read them now, if they should be disinterred from the dust, would be as comic fiction. I infinitely prefer *South Wind*."

J. S. could not but concur with such self-evident truths, and more reluctantly yielded agreement—or half-agreement—to my contention that the main purpose of publishing a book is to have it read, and if it has been continuously read for over thirty years, as *South Wind* has, then a criticism which merely dwells on supposed faults is simply impertinence. "Either," I said, "you have to face the fact that people enjoy what you call 'faults', or else you have to admit that 'faults' don't hamper qualities, and you critics ought to look for the qualities. I take it that all this self-satisfied fault-finding which calls itself 'criticism' is designed first of all to display the superiority of talkers to makers, and after that to help the inferior makers to do better. I wonder if any author ever owed anything positive to critics, ever learned anything from them? And between 1917 and 1947 was there anyone writing or talking 'criticism' competent to give lessons to Norman Douglas?"

I rather had J. S. there, for since he is primarily a 'maker' his author prejudices were naturally flattered by these remarks. Unfortunately, owing no doubt to some glandular deficiency, he cannot refrain from writing 'philosophical' and 'profound' remarks on other peoples'

books for more or less highbrow reviews. So that he
wants to run with the writing hare and hunt with the
critical hounds, and after giving assent to my propositions
he rather inconsistently plunged back into a further
destructive analysis of *South Wind*:

"The plot, if it is a plot," he said, "is simple to the point
of childishness. A Colonial Anglican Bishop proceeding
to England on sick leave calls at the island of Nepenthe to
see his cousin, Mrs. Meadows. She is involved in great
trouble because a blackguard husband who had deserted
her and was presumed dead has suddenly returned and is
trying to blackmail her now that she has found a congenial
lover by whom she has a child. Mrs. Meadows plans and
successfully carries out the murder of her husband, and the
deed is (most improbably and by an awkward device)
witnessed by the Bishop and by him alone. The physical
and moral (or immoral) climate of Nepenthe has in a very
short time so altered the Bishop's views that he condones
the murder. *Voilà tout!*"

I did not then tell J. S., though he will now read it, that
his '*Voilà tout!*' reminded me of a sentence I read in a
Paris students' magazine which announced as an in-
disputable truth that "Voltaire was a bloke (*un type*) who
wrote a couple of pages a day for sixty years—*voilà tout!*"

"Well," J. S. proceeded, not reading my thought,
"there was a theme for an extravaganza or short story of
novelette length if properly constructed, but the author
doesn't know his trade. True, he has created here and
there an ambience and 'atmosphere' of genial and irresponsible paganism, for which I praise him. But about one-
third of his chapters are irrelevant to his theme and therefore from an artistic point of view useless excrescences,
however excellent they may be in themselves as essays.
The author's real problem was admittedly a difficult one,

and, in view of its preposterous nature, the Bishop's
conversion from Christianity to low-class South Italian
immoralism could only take place in an extravaganza.
The Bishop ought to have been shown, by a series of
skilfully-contrived and interwoven incidents and experiences, gradually condoning one by one breaches of
Anglican morals until he arrives at murder . . ."

"But, surely, that is exactly what Douglas has done!"

"You mean that's what he tried to do, but as a matter of
fact through the author's lack of skill these seductive
examples are only presented to the reader, while the
Bishop—for whose benefit they occur—remains blandly
ignorant of them."

"I should like to know where you find them," I said
incredulously.

"I'll give you two examples. The reader (but not the
Bishop) learns that Denis's melancholy and restlessness are
due to his being in love with the Italian ladys'-maid,
Angelina. Like nearly all Douglas's fictional females she is
an unromantic wanton, much the same kind of cynical
sensualist he was himself, in fact, and therefore she
despises the English lad's poetic and respectful devotion,
in spite of his good looks, and yields instantly to the coarse
suggestions of a far from handsome young Jew, who
merely wants to have her and then clear out. Of course,
all things are possible with God and girls, but I suggest to
you that in ninety-nine cases out of a hundred a young girl
(especially an Italian, and therefore at that age intensely
sentimental) would be more likely to prefer the romantic
lover. Let that pass. My point is that this situation, which
might be a solvent of Anglican morality, remains wholly
unknown to the Bishop! The reader is very plainly told,
but the real artistic difficulty was to bring the episode to
the knowledge of the Bishop, and so skilfully that it would

contribute to soften his severity of conscience and
virtuous sitting in judgment on others. It was well-
contrived to make the Bishop sympathise at first with the
drunken but irreclaimable Miss Wilberforce (in using that
name for his drunk Douglas must have remembered
Sheridan in the gutter) for whom nothing could be done,
and censure the young man in his agony of mental and
moral growing pains and the troubles of his first love
affair. What Keith says on this subject is perfectly just.
But the author should have allowed the Bishop to win the
young man's confidence to the extent of discovering his
love for Angelina. Then, after an episcopal but genial talk
on continence, respect for women, sacredness of marriage
and so forth, the Bishop—and not Denis—should have
been the eavesdropper at the Cave of Mercury when
Angelina so improbably yields to young Marten. Then—
but how impossibly difficult this would have been to
anyone but a great genius—we should have to be convinced
that the Bishop was converted to the belief that Angelina
and Marten were perfectly right in their sensual attitude
and behaviour, and Denis a sentimental prig. That indeed
would have been an important step in the Bishop's moral
re-education, and would prepare us for the far more
difficult belief that he would condone a wilful murder."

"I should imagine—judging from the little I know of
modern Christians—that they would prefer to have
murder in the cathedral rather than a love affair in a cave.
But one never knows. What is your other instance?"

"Caloveglia and the forgery of the Locri faun. This,
you'll remember, is carefully worked out by the Count as a
deliberate fraud on his old friend van Koppen, to whom he
sells as an antique the faun he has carved himself in order to
get a dowry for his daughter. The reader of *South Wind* is
shown the whole story, with specious arguments to prove

that there is at least one occasion when the (allegedly) most dignified, honourable and respected man on Nepenthe is justified in perpetrating art frauds—which, by the way, have become distressingly frequent of late years. Of course, van Koppen is allowed to see through the fraud, which he welcomes because it amuses him to see how his English 'art expert' is completely taken in, and because he is delighted to have an opportunity to help his old friend, the Count, with money—Koppen being the only millionaire in history who enjoys being cheated. But this transaction is wholly hidden from the Bishop, who, as a classical scholar, might reasonably have detected the forgery before van Koppen. He might then, after listening to Caloveglia's 'lordly lying', have decided not to expose the old man but to allow him to rob van Koppen in a good cause. Or both could have guessed it, and by an exchange of glances have agreed to keep the secret. At any rate, here is another opportunity lost to sap the Bishop's rigid morals and so take a step nearer to his tolerating, even approving, the enormity of murder. In both these cases the Bishop is a blind attendant on events whose real significance escapes him, and so is not gradually led to the climax. Douglas thinks it sufficient to tell the reader and prepare *him* for the event, and lacks the skill to present these episodes in such a way that the Bishop would understand and be influenced by them."

"Perhaps it was impossible," I suggested.

"If so, that would merely prove that he had chosen an impossible theme," he retorted. "Besides, as in all your English novels of talk, where the personages are not presented as individual characters but as convenient mouthpieces for the expression of various views, the characters of *South Wind* at times are allowed to express themselves in a manner completely contradictory to their

own professions. The Bishop, without adequate pre-
paration, is made to express and to acquiesce in views that
any clergyman would find horribly shocking. Again, the
parroco is introduced to us as 'a rigid disciplinarian . . . a
frost-bitten soul . . . a fighter to the death, a resourceful
ascetic of unbending will . . . a narrow mediæval type
. . . the only person in Nepenthe who would have been
hewn in pieces for his God.' That is clear enough, surely.
The man is a narrow fanatic incapable of formulating any
criticism of his creed. Later in the book the author forgets
about this, and when he is describing the religious
procession headed by the *parroco* under the eruption of
ashes from the volcano, remarks:

'Viewing this cortège of awe-struck innocents braying
into the blackness under their umbrellas at the heels of a
silver-plated idol (not yet paid for) an intelligent God
might well be proud of his workmanship. *So thought the
parroco.*'

"Why did Douglas make such a blunder?" J. S. asked,
again rhetorically. "One can't say definitely, but I should
say that in spite of his later talk about how much work and
thought he put into it, the book was really a light-hearted
and unplanned improvisation from the beginning, and he
never bothered to review it very carefully. See, for
example, how he repeats himself by twice introducing
Mr. Eames with a similar and amusing string of fantastic
misdemeanours Mr. Eames had *not* committed though
gossip on Nepenthe said he had. A careful writer would
have struck out one of them. Why did he make the
parroco think those very thoughts when he, on the author's
own showing, was the one person on the island who would
not think them? The reflection about the intelligent God

is clearly Douglas's. But he had heard from someone supposed to know—perhaps Hueffer?—that the writer of a novel must never make a remark in the first person. Having done so, he tries to hide it by hastily pinning it on the first person who comes to hand, and thereby commits what is supposed to be the even worse fault of omnisciently knowing what is going on in other peoples' minds.

"As to the erudition and the style," J. S. wound up ironically, "they are of course perfect, though it is a pity he makes someone in *South Wind* 'aggravated' when he means 'annoyed' . . . I only hope I haven't 'aggravated' you too much."

7

I HAVE given these views of J. S. on Norman because it is very rarely that we get a French, or at any rate a Continental, judgment on an English-speaking writer from somebody who is really familiar with our language and literature. Moreover, J. S. had evidently made an astonishingly close study of *South Wind* before passing judgment on it—a practice which one could wish, though perhaps not with much hope, to see greatly extended. At any rate, he pointed out to me a number of facts about *South Wind* which I had never noticed, although I have been reading it since it first appeared. Having looked at Wilde for more than half a second I had realised long before Norman's debt to or affinity with Wilde's thought, though I am afraid even his best sayings lack the profundity of Wilde.

How shrewd, for example, is Wilde's saying that one great difference between France and England is that in France every bourgeois wants to be an artist, whereas in England every artist wants to be a bourgeois. On the other hand I was not particularly grateful to J. S. for sharing with me his unflattering discoveries. His remarks tended to confirm my view that critics too often resemble the harpies we read about in Vergil, who snatched away one half of the feast and befouled the rest. Of course, it is regrettable that in *South Wind* Norman wrote 'aggravate' instead of 'annoy'. Out of curiosity I looked up Fowler to see what he says about this usage and read:

> "*Aggravate*, *aggravation*. I. The use of these in the
> sense *annoy*, *vex*, *annoyance*, *vexation*, should be left to the
> uneducated. It is for the most part a feminine or
> childish colloquialism, but intrudes occasionally into
> the newspapers."

Cursedly severe! But other one-time solecisms and
vulgarisms have gained a lawful place in the language,
either through lapse of time or the sanction of some great
writer. Let us hope that Norman's usage will gentle the
condition of 'aggravate'. Like Norman over his dinner, I
am not going to let anyone put me off *South Wind*, which I
value for its gaiety, its cheery irresponsibility, its fantasy,
its defiance of stodgy morals, its recklessness, its amusing
caricatures and intentional absurdities.

Norman has told us that he wrote *South Wind* because
he wanted to get away from "the wearisome actualities of
life" (an escapist, like all genuine artists); and we can well
believe him since the book was written in 1916. A
question for that future biographer to answer or at any
rate to investigate is—had the writing of this book anything to do with Norman Douglas's long exile from
England, which lasted from about 1916 to about 1941? (I
am not sure of the exact dates, but he did not ever visit
England for, roughly, a quarter of a century.) Readers of
the Introduction to *Alone*, with its brilliantly amusing
account of Norman's encounters with upper bureaucrats
in his endeavours to find 'War work', will remember a
particularly virulent attack on "Mr. W——", a young Jew
who had made himself indispensable and hence was
"seated in some comfortable office" while "our own
youngsters" were being destroyed by shell-fire. Why this

bitterness? Norman himself attributes his resolution to
go abroad at that uninviting period to this opposition of
bureaucrats to employing him and to an unspecified
"God-sent little accident, the result of sheer boredom".
But who was "Mr. W——"? Somebody, I forget who,
long ago told me this caricature was meant for Humbert
Wolfe, and this was confirmed in 1934 by the publication
of Wolfe's *Portraits by Inference*. I quote a passage which is a
dialogue between Wolfe and Scott-Moncrieff, whom I
mentioned earlier in this book:

" 'You are perfectly right about my age,' I replied,
'But you know the saying, those whom the gods love die
young, those whom Norman Douglas dislikes are born
old.'

" 'And why did he dislike you?' inquired Scott-
Moncrieff. 'Though, mind you,' he added generously,
'I do not in the least blame him.'

" 'I don't blame him myself. Have you read *Together*?'

" 'It is not a favourite of mine,' said Scott-Moncrieff,
'but I have glanced through it.'

" 'There is a passage,' I said, 'in which Norman
Douglas records how in search of a job during war-time
he was introduced to the room of a certain embusqué.
"A plump, though not ill-looking, young Hebrew was
Mr. W." But it seemed that in spite of his plumpness,
his comparative absence of ugliness, and above all his
Hebraic ancestry he could not "place" Mr. Douglas.
The writer permitted himself to wonder why this
Jewkin was not dispatched to the front.'

" 'And why weren't you?' asked Scott-Moncrieff,
'You were indispensable, I suppose.'

" 'No,' I said, 'merely indistinguishable.'

" 'And because of this incident, wholly discreditable to yourself, you venture to depreciate the author of *South Wind.*'

" 'On the contrary, I adore him. I would almost as soon have written *South Wind* as Shelley's *Ode to the West Wind.* I ventured indeed to dedicate a poem "The Locri Faun" to Mr. Norman Douglas without his permission "from his unknown admirer Mr. W." He never acknowledged it.'

" 'It was probably a very bad poem,' suggested Scott-Moncrieff.

" 'Certainly, I should think.'

" 'But it does not explain why you did not get him a job.'

" 'Well, no—as to that—there was this reason and that reason. It had been indicated to me that at that particular moment in England he would not be a success.' "

The irony of restraint in that last sentence is crushing, for to those who asked him Humbert Wolfe would explain that the reason he could not get Norman Douglas a job was that Wolfe had received a very disagreeable commission from his superiors, namely, to tell Norman that he had the alternative of getting out of England at once or of facing arrest on a certain charge. It was just about the time he published *London Street Games.*

Someone should make a study of The Influence of British Bureaucrats in War-Time on English Literature. The same people who expelled Norman, who wanted to stay in England and work for them, refused a passport to Lawrence, who wouldn't work for them and wanted to leave England. They scotched but did not kill *The Rainbow*, but may they not have stimulated the production of *South Wind* from a high-spirited, vindictive man whom they tried to crush, just as in a different way they tried to crush Lawrence? Yet, with the conspicuous exception of France, and in spite of the dishonest misuse of the laws of libel and obscenity, there is probably still more liberty for independent writers in England than elsewhere. A discouraging thought. With how much graver anxiety and more wistful irony may we echo Wordsworth's:

"Oh grief that Earth's best hopes rest all with Thee!"

With the exception of *Together*, which is concerned with his childhood's Vorarlberg, I should say that almost all Norman's best writing is set in Southern Italy, in or about his siren land which includes Nepenthe and can easily be linked with the two travel books (*Old Calabria* and *Alone*) and the *Capri Materials*. It is surely one of Norman's achievements that he was able to give such distinction and even an illusion of originality to an area so hackneyed and for so long tourist-ridden as the Gulf of Naples and Capri? How was it done? Well, he had a rare combination of energies and interests—sea excursions and long wanderings afoot, local friendships, scholarly collections, prolonged studies among documents in the libraries of Naples and Cava, enthusiasms for geology, natural history, botany, afforestation, old customs, out-of-the-way history, departed manners. Probably there were more reasons than one for the abandonment of that projected great work on Capri. I ought to have among my letters from him something to add to those Capri notes, but all I find is the following, dated 28th May, 1932, when I was staying at Anacapri:

"Dear Richard,

Thank you for your card. That was very brilliant of B. to get up Monte Solaro! Go some cloudless evening there, and have a look at the Ponza island and Capo Circello. As to orchids—now is the time for the *homme-pendu* species, but they are rather difficult to see, on account of their very insignificant colour. Very sorry to hear about the red lilies. On the 20th June they should be in blossom. You can get a useful map of Capri on the spot: it is marked Prop. Art. Lett. *Gianotti* at bottom right hand.

N."

Well, I had seen Ponza and Capo Circello from the top of Monte Solaro as far back as the spring of 1913, which was the happiest of my life. I don't remember what was the complaint about red lilies, but I think I must have groused to him about the destruction of wild flowers between 1913 and 1932 all along the Migliara path. What had been a paradise of lovely southern wild flowers had been turned into a desert of ugly scraggly little 'cultivated' patches. Nooks and tiny fields, where in 1913 you could find wild violets, snowflake, anemones and wild gladiolus, had been denuded, and lay cracked and parched in the sun, bearing a thin, stunted, withered crop of oats some six inches high, utterly useless, a monument of human stupidity, delusive additions to department of agriculture statistics of 'areas newly planted with cereals'. When I first was on Capri I had with me a copy of Theocritus, and was astonished to discover on the island so many of the flowers and wild things he mentions in Sicily. I wonder how many can be found now. Europe is now a discouraging place for those who 'love green haunts and loneliness'. Scarcely have you discovered a rare nook when along comes government enterprise with a bull-dozer to destroy it for some perverse and maniac purpose. No wonder Norman hated both goats and governments, and braved the discomforts of Calabria to get away from utilitarian destructions.

I think I can add one tiny detail of Capri lore to Norman's collection. In *Late Harvest* he refers (apparently as something he had lately learned) to the story of Sir Nathaniel T——, who made a fortune in Italy by selling the Italians dried codfish, and built himself the Palazzo Inglese on Capri about the middle of the eighteenth century. T—— obviously stands for Thorold, for the name is given in full in Harold Trower's *The Book of Capri*, which refers the reader to Stamer's *Dolce Napoli* for more details. I have not read this book, but heard the story forty years ago from Mr. Algar Thorold, a descendant. In Norman's version when the family asked that Sir Nathaniel's body should be sent to England, it could not be found, and a sailor's was substituted. According to Mr. Thorold, his ancestor was an Admiral, and the body sent was that of a Capri hermit, while the heretic Admiral was buried in place of the hermit. I seem to remember, but cannot vouch for it, that the buried Admiral wrought miracles and was beatified. This is surely the better version, and the one Norman should have preferred.

I don't think I bought the map of Capri to which Norman refers. The one I found useful, and still by chance possess, is that attached to Harold Trower's *The Book of Capri*, 2nd edition, 1924. Those who have read the long footnote on pp 261–2 of *Capri Materials*, where Norman points out the shortcomings of Gianotti's map, will wonder why Norman failed to recommend the map in Trower's book, which contains the matter omitted by Gianotti, and had been available for several years when

L

Norman recommended it to me in 1932. Can it be that he did not know of it? Of course he knew of it! The first edition of Trower's book appeared at the significant date of 1906, just at the time when Norman abandoned his own projected book on Capri. The second edition, with the excellent map, appeared in 1924, and that or a later edition was on sale when I was last in Capri, in 1936.

The fact is that we here stumble on one of Norman's personal and literary feuds, the most violent of which was with D. H. Lawrence. If we turn up Mr. King's *South Wind* Introduction we shall discover that the unflattering portraits of Freddy Parker and his 'lady' were intended for Mr. and Mrs. Trower—in Norman's own words "a particularly objectionable pair of English residents" (of Capri) who "could have been recognised from my sketch, as I meant them to be." Again, the character of Malipizzo was intended for Capolazzi, the magistrate of Capri who, again according to Norman, twice "nearly had me in the lock-up." Since Trower was British Consular Agent on Capri, there is a possibility that he may have had something to do with these near lock-up incidents. At any rate, he must have known about them, and it may even have been his duty to report on them to London. Anyway, here is the self-confessed fact that Freddy Parker was meant for Harold Trower, whose rival book on Capri is nowhere mentioned in Norman's writings.

In his Introduction Mr. King tells us that he bought (second-hand) a copy of the 1906 edition of Trower's *The Book of Capri*, and adds that, "unlike *South Wind*," it is "completely unreadable." Now, this comparison strikes me as unrealistic and unfair. *The Book of Capri* is not a novel, and makes no pretensions to being a work of art or of entertainment. It is a historical and general guide to Capri, and if it is to be compared with any of Norman's writings it should be not with *South Wind* but with the *Capri Materials*. Unlike the last-mentioned work, *The Book of Capri* was completed, and, to the best of my belief, preceded all Norman's publications on Capri except for the articles on the *Blue Grotto* and on *Forestal Conditions*. Four other Douglas articles on Capri were published in the same year as Trower's book. As the original edition of that book contained about forty chapters or articles, each on a different topic, priority of publication must be allowed in nearly all cases to Trower. There is no escape from it.

That Mr. King could find only a second-hand copy of a book which (except for the period 1922–24) was in print from 1906 to 1939 was either a misfortune or a piece of luck. That he found the book 'completely' unreadable suggests a perusal as hasty as his reading of Wilde, since the notes on the *Blue Grotto* are derived and quoted (with acknowledgments) from Norman's article. The chapter on Capri geology was written by the Italian specialist, Dr. Cerio, who is quoted twelve times in *Capri Materials*. The chapter on ancient marbles comes from Pullen and Lanciani, and so forth. However dull, it is more informative than anything on the topic in *Capri Materials*, and so are the notes on Roman building materials and on Capri in the Middle Ages. Of course Norman's article on Tiberius is immeasurably better written than Trower's, but contains much the same information (Trower is more complete) and comes to much the same conclusion— indeed a rehabilitation of Tiberius in 1906 was knocking down an open door, since the change of opinion was started by Voltaire. Which of the two has priority in the account of the French and British occupation of Capri during the Napoleonic Wars? In any event, Trower's is fuller and more documented. Their respective bibliographies show that they consulted the same authorities, each having a few the other lacks. However inferior from a literary point of view, Trower's book contained so much of the available material that there was not room for another English book on Capri; and one cannot help thinking that it was mainly the publication of *The Book of Capri* which checked Norman's studies and writings on the subject. Significantly his last separate complete article on Capri was published in January, 1907, the life of Suor Serafina which he later summarised (and improved) for *Siren Land*. Thereafter he issued only the *Antiquarian Notes*, the *Disjecta Membra*, and the *Index*.

To make a fair comparison of *The Book of Capri* and *Materials for a Description of Capri* we have to consider the equipment and intentions of the two writers. Trower was a man of some culture (Balliol and Inns of Court) who set out to provide a popular historical and topographical guide to Capri, calling on real or supposed experts (e.g. Cerio, and later Günther and Cuomo) for chapters on their specialities. He was probably at work on his book long before Norman went to live on Capri in 1902, since two of Trower's chapters appeared in English periodicals during 1903. Nobody in his senses would think of putting Trower in the same literary class as Douglas, yet he succeeded in his modest task better than one would have expected after hearing him called 'unreadable'. It is impossible to say what Norman planned, but even he would have been hard put to it to make a really attractive and entertaining book out of the hackneyed and dry-as-dust Capri material. Perhaps Norman meditated a scholarly book in the German manner, though for all his researches he admits that he had been able to add very little fresh knowledge to the stock.

A good deal more of the *Capri Materials* has been incorporated in Norman's other writings than his preface indicates. I think he over-depreciates the book in *Late*

Harvest when he says that nobody would succeed in reading it and that it is only 'for reference'. I know I am not the only person who has read *Capri Materials* more than once from beginning to end, and with pleasure; but perhaps that calls for a special interest both in Capri and in Norman Douglas. Who can read, for instance, the reprint of Fabio Giordano and Norman's copious commentary without thinking of Mr. Eames and his annotations to Monsignor Perelli?

I find only one other reference to Capri in my surviving letters from Norman, and that only a passing one. Under date 23rd August, 1932 he wrote:

"My dear Richard,

So glad to get yours of the 19th. I don't wonder at your being sick of Capri, I wonder at your having stood it so long. A fortnight at a time is my maximum nowadays! But anyway you were getting through with your novel, and I hope you will have no trouble with the tail-end of it.

We had a lovely time in Austria. The weather happened to be good (which occurs about once in ten years) and I think Charles and Pino enjoyed themselves properly. I am rather sorry I returned so soon. The day after they went a son of mine turned up, and not alone, else we two could have done a little climbing.

Here it is *grilling* hot.

Brantôme sounds an ideal spot for writing in. I passed through that district in 1889, on a high bicycle, but haven't been there since.

Reggie in Switzerland; Pino, presumably, downstairs, working on his catalogue. Endless love to B. and to Frere.

Yours ever,

Norman."

Probably it is a very recent re-reading of Norman's notes to Fabio Giordano which makes me feel that I could write a long commentary on that letter. How much one could write about the topic of living on Capri, let alone the other aspects of Norman's life glanced at or implied in that letter! I shall use self-restraint and limit myself to one little footnote on Anacapri, which I don't remember to have seen mentioned either by Norman or anyone else. Throughout the year, but especially in the heat-burdened silence of summer days, the church clock perpetually chimes—or used to chime—the first three notes of Grieg's *Er ist tod*. I used to wonder why, until I discovered that Grieg lived on Anacapri while writing part of the Peer Gynt suite, and that endlessly repeated 'da—dee—da' found its way into his music.

The casual reference to the "lovely time in Vorarlberg" makes me regret more than ever that, as I was travelling, I missed most of the cards and letters they all sent me. It must have been Pinorman's first meeting with Charles after his generous payment for *Looking Back*, and the ensuing celebrations must have been worth recording. I find no trace of them, and though it is a digression I am tempted to fill the gap with passages from some of Charles's letters when, on another occasion, he was hoping to take his partner, Ian Parsons, to Vorarlberg when there descended on him a flight of those actions for technical libel which the English Courts so sedulously fostered in those days. It was one of the classic methods by which the legal profession visited its dislike and envy on the literary profession:

"We had settled X—," Charles wrote, "and life seemed to be reasonably harmonious once more, when crash! a bomb from another quarter. . . . Counsel is sitting on the damn thing at the moment. This is the foulest luck, and Ian and I are as sick as mud, since we may quite well be kept from Austria. This morning too a letter from Pino in which, not yet knowing that the X— business had been settled, he declared that he and Norman would not go to Austria unless we were able to join them—which consternates me, as I know how eager Norman is to get up into the ancestral mountains. However, there is still a chance, though rather a thin one."

On the back of this letter is added the following out-burst—most rare from the gentle Charles—dated the next day:

"Interrupted yesterday evening by a letter sent down from our lawyers with Counsel's opinion, from which, according to the familiar recipe, followed other letters, telephone conversations, etc. More again this morning. But what infuriates me is that I've just had a wire from Norman and Pino saying they are stopping in Florence. Isn't it just ———— you know what, fill in the missing word to suit. However, Counsel doesn't think the Y— business is serious (as indeed I could hardly think myself) and we may be just able to nip off to Vorarlberg yet and join hands there with Pinorman."

Four days later Charles wrote that "it looks as if Ian and I, thanks to Harold's generosity, will be able to hop off to Austria on Thursday afternoon," adding that he would certainly adopt my suggestion and address a mountaineering Pino "by the name of MacAlpino—especially as one of my grandmothers was called MacAlpine." Alas for Charles's holiday! Only two days after this came yet another threat of libel! This time Charles was really disgusted. It was 'despicable', 'the limit'. In answer to my expressions of concern at this cascade of persecutions —which made me think of those night-time libations from above into the streets of eighteenth-century Edinburgh— he added:

"Don't feel worried about us. We are all right—only extremely annoyed (to put it mildly) at missing our train this afternoon. Think of it! Kept from Norman and Pino by Messrs Y— and K—!!!"

Think of it indeed. I should say that the libels might have been settled both ways by the champions at the expense of a little back-hair-pulling and screaming.

Returning to Charles's 1932 meeting with Pinorman in Vorarlberg—I have just turned up a letter from Pino dated from Thüringen, 6th August, 1932, in which he details some of his preparations for an appropriate reception:

"My dearests,
Charles arriving today. Norman and I we shall do our best to make him drunk so to forget the terrible time he had.
I am so pleased you have done so much work. I am longing to see it finished. I still go on without smoking, but since in Austria I have given away to wine and I do drink." [I bet he did!] "it is such a change after 2 month of abstemy.
"I wish you were both here with us to receive Charles to-day, what a time we should have. I am putting my best clothes on. a cordaroy complete which I had made in Florence on purpose for Charles, a bright yellow shirt with a blue tie, I look a real ——. Charles' room is full of shealling-waxe, flowers and kind of

charms against the W.W. I hope Charles will write to you and describe our pub. The W.C. is the most comfortable primitive one, two people can do at the same time. I am keeping a diary in English, this time is most pure, full of impotency on the part of N.D. I have been working in the rainy days at my C.L.S. book.

all my love to you both,

Pino."

Pino's letter cries for a commentary. The W.W. was the Woolley-Woolley (alias Voolley-Voolley) a mythical Normanian monster of Vorarlberg, which haunted a stretch of country between Feldkirch and Bludenz, and had to be placated with gifts and offerings of flowers, and sealing-wax and I know not what else. If I lie, call me horse, spit in my face, but having neglected these offerings in disdain of superstition, I had my car smashed and was myself crippled on that very stretch of road in an accident due to a front-tyre blow-out in a car coming towards me. When I add that the driver's name was Dökkls, and that the German for Douglas is Döggls. . . . I remember that corduroy 'complete' of Pino's, and he undoubtedly went to endless trouble and some expense to dress up for Charles's amusement. 'Abstemy' is a very nice word, which I hope that some day the successors of the great Fowler will permit us to use, though in Pino's case I suggest that 'waggonising' might be more expressive. The C.L.S. book must have been the draft of *Moving Along* which Norman re-wrote—how much I should like to see the original!

Under the sway of memory and these old letters I have diverged so far from *Capri Materials* that the reader will by now have forgotten about them. I question whether anything of the slightest literary interest in them has been wasted by not being used elsewhere. *Suor Serafina*, *Tiberius*, *The Blue Grotto*, *Forestal Conditions* all turn up, almost verbatim, in other books; for though Norman had many specialist interests, his literary equipment was more modest than you would suppose, especially from the impression he skilfully created of having always a great deal of strength in reserve. Perhaps he had, but he never brought it into action. He made admirable use of the materials he had. Indeed, he used them over and over again, and I think no writer of his status and reputation has so much duplicated and padded his later books as Norman. Nobody writing for many years can wholly avoid this, but he should at least try to get permission from the publisher to whom he first sold the copyright.

Consider that admirable *Typhoeus* essay which was chopped up and distributed among other essays of *Siren Land*, the copyright in which had gone to Martin Secker. Around 1930–31 Norman was trying to re-sell it and his article on the Ponza Islands. I find a letter of November, 1931, from Charles says:

"I am glad you reassured Norman about *Paneros*; I am certain we are going to get home on it, and I'm happy that America has taken it too. I haven't seen his *Summer Islands;* I suppose they are the essays on Ponza etc. from the *English Review* he once suggested for *Three of Them*, and I replied that I rather felt their publication would infringe Secker's copyright."

I'd say it would! But either Secker's permission was obtained or he was magnanimous (I suspect the latter), for he did not assert his rights when *Typhoeus* and the Ponza Islands were re-issued in the 1930s. In 1942 forty-five copies of the same text were issued by the Corvinus Press

(Carlow); and in 1946 *Late Harvest* again reprinted the article and passages from *Typhoeus*, with no acknowledgment to Secker. Thrift! The wedding baked-meats did duty at the funeral. Consider *Late Harvest*, which was put out as a 'new' book. It runs to 125 pages, and the whole of pages 79–125 consists of reprints of these Islands essays and miscellaneous work from *The English Review* which had already been issued in the stupidly-titled *Experiments*. Parts of the earlier pages have been transferred from *Looking Back*. Again, the whole of the Introduction to that book of Capri photographs is repetition except for two or three paragraphs. Norman has written—and I have heard him discourse, with 'meaning glances'—on the crime of 'literary diarrhœa' and the supreme merit of 'lying fallow'. He seems to have lain fallow for twenty years. I could wish he had displayed the candour of Samuel Butler, who said:

"Perhaps it is better that I should not have a chance of becoming a hack writer, for I should grasp it at once if it were offered me."

And, as a matter of fact, to do him justice, I believe Norman did grasp at any such chance when it came his way. *Late Harvest*, among other objectives, aims at anticipating or rebutting certain inevitable posthumous criticisms; and therein Norman gives his version of the commission he sought and was granted which led to the writing of *One Day*. Representations having been made to them, the none too opulent Greek government gave him £300 and what are known as 'facilities' to write a *book* about Greece on the lines of *Old Calabria*. Norman was given a free run of the excellent library belonging to the British School at Athens, and very soon realised that if he was to do a book on the scale of *Old Calabria* he would not only have to do some travelling but a great deal of reading. He recoiled from the labour, and produced as his part of the contract nothing but the fifty-pages essay called *One Day*. It is a very good essay, in fact the only readable portion of *Three of Them*, which is padded out to 239 pages by the inclusion of a feeble, sort of *Horla* story called *Nerinda*, and his boyish disquisition on the lizards, snakes, toads, newts and frogs of Baden. But what about the book which he had promised to produce? Well, he excuses his failure by a calculation that his fifty-page essay had cost the Greek taxpayers only a fraction of a farthing per head (you could excuse Unesco or any other —— on the same lines) and modestly describes his fifty pages as:

". . . . a book not imposing perhaps as to bulk, but crammed with shrewd and suggestive observations, exhaling a candid love of their race and fatherland and a reverence for its traditions, a book written by a country-man of their hero, Byron, and in a style, moreover, which no critic will call displeasing: all this for the fraction of a farthing!"

No! For three hundred pounds. Passing lightly over the fact that a fair proportion of the 'candid love' is concentrated on schoolboys, I should like to point out one or two facts. If Norman did not write a full-length *Old Hellas* it was either because he wouldn't or he couldn't, either because he was indolent or because he hadn't the knowledge—which latter indeed he half confesses was the fact. As to the fraction of a farthing argument—who can doubt that if the thumb-screwed Greek tax-payers had been asked whether they wanted that sum of drachmas wasted on a mere bit of writing they would have risen

from their Schedule A's like one man to thunder: *No!*
Further, when you have contracted to write a book on the
lines of one which contains forty short essays, you can
hardly claim to have honoured your bond by producing
one essay of fifty pages. (First edition of *Old Calabria* has
322.) Few devotees of art, even when subsidised by
public money, would feel satisfied if an architect who had
contracted to produce a mansion should put up a handsome entrance hall and then claim he was a public
benefactor and countryman of Lord Byron, not to mention
Bailie MacBawbee of Aberdeen.

Of course, if it were possible to express literary merit
in terms of money—which it isn't—one could argue that
such an essay was well worth 300 pounds. I think it was.
But that is as irrelevant as Norman's argument about the
imperceptible burden he placed on the Greek tax-
payer. The point is that if you contract to produce a book
of essays and produce only one essay you haven't fulfilled
your side of a bargain.

If Charles felt that the two *Summer Islands* essays were a
violation of Secker's copyright, I wonder what he would
have said of *Capri Materials*? If anyone doubts the
duplication of the books, let him compare the duplicate
essays on *Tiberius* and on *The Blue Grotto* and the two lives
of *Suor Serafina*. They are virtually identical, and if
Secker's permission was obtained for this reprint of work
which had been leased to him no acknowledgment of it
appears in the book. All of which goes to show the
advantage of being a gentleman author and not a mere
hack.

8

AFTER the autumn of 1932 I find my 'Pinormaniana',
as Charles used to call them, less plentiful. Partly this
was because I had by then heard most of Pino's stories,
partly because I went less often to Italy, and was away for
long periods in the West Indies and United States. And
because of a wandering life there are many gaps in letters
preserved, even those from Charles. It is a letter of his,
dated November, 1932, and sent to me in Portugal, which
contains these significant words:

> "Send Norman a card if you've time. Pino has been
> Reggie-fying, and he (Norman) sounds very gloomy—
> cursing Italian cooking and bloodying Chianti like mad.
> And I've heard nothing from Pino either for days. An
> acute attack of Reggie-itis!"

Of course, there were times when Pino rebelled against
Norman's too obvious dominion over him or against
something Pino considered an outrage. As I have mentioned, they had a private speaking-tube between their
flats, as Norman feared that he might be taken ill and die
without anyone knowing; though needless to say he out-
lived his junior by more than a decade.

On the other hand, there were times when Norman was
angry with Pino, and very often the cause was that
mentioned in Charles's letter, i.e. an attack of Reggie-itis.

Although Norman used all his powers of persuasion and invective—which were very considerable—to prove that Reggie's 20,000 pounds bequest to Pino was a pure illusion, he never carried conviction. I have an idea that Pino had seen the will, so that whenever Reggie chose to shake it Pino felt he had to run off and cultivate him— which left Norman lonely. Attempts to settle the problem by getting Reggie to dine with us nearly always failed. The scene between James Argyle (Norman) and Algy Constable (Reggie) in *Aaron's Rod* gives a very typical instance of how they could not be kept from bickering and so spoiling the evening. Of course, Norman was quite right. There was no reason at all why a man of his eminence should put up with Reggie. After such encounters, Pino, as likely as not, had a revulsion of feeling and began spending time with Norman, until once more the shaking of the will brought him to heel. Towards the end of 1933 there were rumours that Reggie was seriously threatening to alter his will and leave everything to his Italian servants.

The reference to Ouida and her essays in the following letter from Norman needs explanation. By this time it seemed plain that Norman was completely written out and had literally nothing more to say, and Charles and I tried to think of a book or books which Norman would supposedly edit (we could do that for him) and for which he could write an Introduction as short as he pleased, but be paid. Waterton, however, was in Everyman; Ramage, Charles thought, was not for our epoch; but he thought there might be a chance of Ouida's *Essays* (which Norman had praised), the copyright of which belonged to Chatto's. Nothing came of the plan, I suppose because of the public prejudice worked up against Ouida.

"Florence

28 Feb 1934

"My dear Richard,

Very glad to get yours of the 16th and to know that you are all right again. I also had a stiff dose of influenza, and at this moment Pino is laid up with inflammation of the parotid gland; he is very much better, but mayn't go out yet. Not that one is very much tempted to do so! The weather is viler than it need be, and I am getting sick of this blasted winter.

As to forwarding your letters from Cooks'—no trouble at all.

And as to Ouida—I think some of her essays, say about half (which would make a single volume) would be worth re-printing: they are certainly worth re-reading. And yet I doubt whether it would be anything but a loss to a publisher. Elizabeth Lee is—or rather was (I hope) —a ————— ———. But I gave it her hot in the *English Review*, when that book of hers came out; and also to Henry James and his opinions of Ouida, in *Alone*.

The only news here is of the smash of XXXXXX Bank; I daresay you have heard of it. The place has now been closed for over a fortnight. Nearly all the Anglo-American colony, as well as heaps of Italians, had money deposited there; Pino and Reggie are hard hit. They say they may get a percentage of it back, but nobody knows anything definite. A bloody mess anyhow.

Much love to B.

Yours ever

Norman."

I had to look up 'parotid gland' in the *Encyclopædia* to find out what it is and what can go wrong with it. After that I spent a restless night worrying about Pino, sick and disconsolate and hard up, with Reggie who might have helped him evidently short of whatever he had in his current account. Pino must somehow get some cash to maintain his flat and carry on his business until he could get out a new catalogue or the Bank paid something to its creditors. It was painful indeed to think of Pino perhaps deprived even of his 'vine'! In those days I had a theory—which, as a matter of fact, I still hold—that if a hack writer has any money he should invest it in his friends and not in the debt of governments or pernicious 'industries'. So, hoping it might help a little, I sent Pino a cheque for a hundred pounds, and was more than repaid by the following letter:

"Firenze
7th March 1934

"My dearest Richard,

I have been to Montecatini with my brother-in-law for the week-end and only yesterday I found your letter with the contents. You are too generous and too good to me, and I have no words for thanking you. I only wished you had been here when I open your letter and I should have jumped to your neck and kissed you. I shall never, never forget your spontaneous act of generosity and you will have my gratitude for ever and ever.

It has been a terrible blow to me, as if the XXXX really goes (which we hope not) I shall have lost all my economies. Reggie is in it for a very considerable sum over 450,000.

Now everyone seem optimistic about it, and it is true it seems that the government is going to take the all affair in hand and they say that every one is going to be

M

paid. If so (let us hope) it will be my first thought to repay you back the sum which so generously you have sent me. If not, I shall keep it as a loan, and I will certainly repay you in time.

Again and again my dearest Richard I thank you for your sympathy and help in this distressing moment. Give my love to dear B. and a lot for you

from yours ever

Pino."

And that was the last I heard of it. What says the Good Book? *"Nous promettons selon nos espérances et nous tenons selon nos craintes"*—a foolish remark, which is equally true if stood on its head. Dear Pino.

My experience of life teaches me that he who lives on and on in hopes of a legacy dooms himself to a life of depressing misery. My thanks to whatever gods may be that on the occasion when I was threatened with such 'Greek gifts' I was always inspired so to behave that I was speedily cut out with execrations. What slavery is like unto that extracted from his obsequious legatee by a churlish money-bags? (Look up Martial and Petronius.) Still, poor Pino had more than his fair share of servitude in earning Reggie's 20,000 pounds, which anyway came to him too late to be a real compensation.

The end of this story is contained in two letters written to me from France by Norman after he had to fly from Italy in 1937. Before quoting those letters I should say that in the summer of 1938 I received a letter from Reggie, rather a sad one, congratulating me on the birth of my daughter, "the only real immortality". I did not know then how far gone he was with that dreadful disease, cancer of the tongue. Suddenly came a telegram from Pino to say Reggie was dead, whereupon I cabled him money to lay a

wreath from me on Reggie's tomb—I think the only one I
have ever sent in my life. Why did I waste money on what
I then thought and still think an absurd superstition and a
profanation of beautiful flowers, which should be devoted
to feasts and youth and the courtship of women? Well,
somehow Pino had found out that Reggie, although poor,
had denied himself to send a wreath to the funeral of Oscar
Wilde. And we agreed that Reggie had deserved well of
the Republic of Letters, that though a despised Jew he had
been courageous in standing by a fallen hero, and, in short,
that if Reggie pre-deceased us we would each send his
funeral the best wreath we could afford, with the same
inscription he had put on his to Wilde. Pino assured me it
was done, both for his wreath and mine.

> "Monaco A.M.
>
> 19 Dec 1938

"My dear Richard,

Very glad to get yours of the 12th.

As to Reggie—he died on the 7th. A relief for
everybody including himself, as he seems to have
suffered terribly. I had a *wire* to that effect from Pino,
who has not written me a line for two months. Why?

No. I shall hang on here quietly over Christmas, and
will be glad when that ridiculous business is over.

> always
>
> Norman."

It took Norman not to see that the reason Pino hadn't
written to any of us was because he was shattered and
exhausted by waiting on Reggie's death-bed. Pino was
vulnerable as a woman without a woman's unselfish
strength. Now here comes the next phase of Pino's
savage pilgrimage in search of a fortune:

"Monaco A.M.

13 Jan 1939

"My dear Richard,

. . . Pino writes that he must now leave for England on account of Reggie's will, but he can't come through France as the Italians will not give him a French visa. What a state of affairs! But everybody is going mad, anyway. As to Archie—he is at Vence again. I met him the other day and we dined together at Antibes. XYZ has been rather ill lately, but a severe non-alcoholic dietary is working wonders.

How is your writing getting on? I am reading Enid Starkie's Life of Rimbaud—very interesting; she has got hold of some new material.

Yours ever

Norman."

By the time that letter was posted I was on the way to America, and thereafter my only news of Pino was by letters and they all appear to have been lost. My recollection is that, as indicated in Norman's letter, Pino went to London on a binge to try to forget the horrors of Reggie's lingering death. He then spent months entangled in the law's delays, trying to get possession of the money left to him, and just about the time he got it another war started which left him in an awkward position. True, Italy was not at that time in the war, but there was always the risk, and Pino might have had his newly-acquired English money 'conveyed' by a high-souled government. On the other hand if he stayed in England he was likely to be interned. So Pino fled to Portugal, whether with or without his legacy I never knew, nor how and when he died except that he did die there. At that time so many private letters between America and Europe were lost that

at last one gave up writing in despair. That war was the
end of all our merry times and friendship.

The death of Pino seems to have been a bad business,
and that future biographer should look into it and try to
find out what really happened. Strangely enough, thinking
Pino would be safe either in England or Italy I was much
more concerned at that time about Norman, and I have
memories of a correspondence with Mr. Robin Douglas in
which we tried to devise some plan whereby his father
could come over and live with him. I shall always regret
that this failed, partly because it would certainly have
averted a fatal misunderstanding which arose because
impossibilities (almost) of communication prevented my
showing him a piece of writing about him before
publication, as I should have done otherwise; and partly
because I think the shock of that different landscape and
civilisation might have given him just the stimulus needed
to bring him out of the sterility of his later years. So far
as my knowledge goes, Norman always got on well with
Americans and had insuperable and ridiculous prejudices
against America. Of course, closer and more accurate
information might in his case merely have resulted in a
premature air-conditioned nightmare, but the experiment
should have been made.

Another tangle or series of tangles which that biographer will have to try to clear up is the Maurice Magnus
affair. I touched briefly on this awkward topic in a
volume of reminiscences (published only in America) and
in a life of Lawrence, but as it led directly to a breach
between Norman and myself I can't omit it from these
pages. Though to that extent a party, I shall try to give my
evidence as carefully as if I were on oath in a Court of Law.
If that sounds portentous, let me say that warfare between
two such free spirits and great writers as Norman Douglas

and D. H. Lawrence was a misfortune for both literature and themselves. That Magnus pamphlet was by far the cleverest and most damaging attack made on Lawrence, and did him more harm than he realised. Most of Lawrence's other enemies were men of straw whose words vanished in a month, but Norman Douglas was a very different matter. In the first place he had known Lawrence on and off for twenty years, and what he wrote was sure to remain and to be taken seriously. Moreover, Pino, who to my certain knowledge had been enthusiastically pro-Lawrence in 1930, came over (seemingly) so whole-heartedly to Norman's views that the passages in Pino's two books referring to Lawrence might have been written —and in my opinion were written—by Norman himself. To those who don't know the inside of the story, that looks as if Norman had a very valuable witness. In his life-time Lawrence, conscious of his own good intentions toward Magnus and that he was guiltless of what befel the man through his own imprudence and worse, made no reply except by a very effective but belated letter to *The New Statesman*. But naturally that was soon forgotten until it was reprinted in *Phoenix* and later in the *Selected Essays* of the Penguin Lawrence. I have been trying for years, without success, to get a reprint of Lawrence's original essay on Magnus, not only because it contains very fine writing but because it is obviously the truth. I must ask the reader's indulgence if I relate this story, and my own unforeseen entanglement with it, in my own way. As I keep no diary and have lost letters and documents which I need for precision I have to rely on fallible memory, and my dates can only be approximate.

Early in 1939 I was in New York, and just about that time the American branch of the Oxford University Press published an edition of *Old Calabria* in The World's

Classics. This was done by my friend, Paul Willert, then head of the O.U.P. in America, not with any hope of big sales but because of his admiration for Norman's books. Of course, it is a compliment to a living writer, and was so meant, to include him in The World's Classics; though I must admit Norman's slight comment on this edition shows no very lively sense of his having been complimented. It must have been from Mr. Willert I learned that the venture had been a most dismal failure. At that time I had given up reviewing for years, and my belief is that I had not been able to write anything in praise of Norman's books for six or seven years. But when I was given the opportunity to write about *Old Calabria* for *The Atlantic Monthly* I was glad to accept. At any rate, as the reader will have seen from my account of the journey with Pino and Charles, I had seen something of the country and had been reading and re-reading the book for twenty years. I forgot whose idea it was that I should try to attract attention to the book through the author by giving some account of Norman. Of course, I ought to have asked his permission, but conditions made it very difficult, and I tried (however unsuccessfully) to make the review what Strachey called a "portrait in miniature" with some impressions and anecdotes of the author. A copy of the *Atlantic* was, I believe, sent to Norman, and probably I wrote a letter of explanation. Some months later I was greatly pleased to receive from Norman the following charming note:

"I Place Macé
Antibes A.M.
24 July 1939

"My dear Richard,
I have just run into Frere—or rather, he has run into

me—and that reminds me that I never thanked you for writing that admirable article (far too flattering, of course, but why not?) about me. But I am sorry to hear from Frere that you think of *staying* in America. What is this? Please drop me a line, and say when you are coming back to Europe. I haven't seen you since Canadel, *and want to see you again.*

Always
Norman"

(The italics are N.D.'s)

I must have answered so pleasant a letter, though I have forgotten what I said, but the point is that it certainly seemed to me to express a friendly feeling for myself and an assurance that I had not done wrong in what I had written about him. I leave it to the reader to judge whether, after such a letter, I was or was not justified in thinking he would not be displeased if I took advantage of some future opportunity to try to be of service to him in a similar way.

Such an opportunity came up some months to a year later. I had to write one or two articles for the magazine *Esquire*, which specialises in what they imagine to be men's men and interests. It was, so to speak, a Ganders Only vehicle, and the difficulty was to find suitable subjects. It suddenly occurred to me that Norman with his out-of-doors life and interests, his shooting chamois and mountaineering and yachting, his journeys in Tunisia, India and Tanganyika, his Calabrian wanderings, even his prowess at table, would make an excellent subject. Now, the intensification of the war made it impossible for me to submit the article to him (I didn't know where he was), but as he had approved so heartily of the former effort to serve him I felt confident he would not disapprove of this one. I have lost that article, and all I can learn about it comes from Mr. Cecil Woolf (Norman's bibliographer), who tells me the exact title under which it was published. This was not my title, and it is certainly vulgar and silly. I had never heard of it, and can only suppose that, as I was very busy with other literary work at the time, I never looked at the article after I had passed the proofs.

The next thing was that this article appeared in some small London periodical, whose name I have now forgotten, without my knowledge or permission or any payment to me—though possibly my London agent had given permission and the letter telling me vanished with so many others.

In view of the approval of my former article as expressed in Norman's letter of July, 1939, I think I had every reason to suppose that he would approve the *Esquire* article, since it was equally enthusiastic about him and his books. Judge then of my astonishment and anger when a letter came through from England containing a cutting from the periodical which had 'conveyed' (so far as I know) my article. This was a letter from Norman to the editor, written in his most offensive, fine-old-Scottish-gentleman style, blackguarding me and my article which he kindly described as "American nonsense"! Considering that I had taken time off from much more profitable work to try and give his American sales a boost this seemed harsh treatment, especially as I was not conscious of having said anything to offend him. I am vain, quick-tempered and impatient. I think now that what I should have done was to write Norman (but I had no address) and ask what was the trouble. I didn't. I damned his impudence, screwed up the cutting and threw it in the waste-paper basket. And that was that.

Now what had I said, to be smitten by this unfriendly

fulmination when I imagined that at least I was earning a few lines of approval on Café notepaper? At the time and for years afterwards (if I ever thought of it, which I did not) I had no idea. Only recently have I begun to discover what the crime was. When *Late Harvest* came out, or soon afterwards, I bought a copy to keep the home fires burning, but only glanced at it because I soon saw it was mostly a re-hash of material I had read before. Only just lately have I discovered that my offence was in taking Lawrence's side in that ridiculous Magnus business. And, though Norman denounced the English reprint of my *Esquire* article, I really don't think that was the cause of the trouble, unless indeed I repeated there what I said in a book (which I shall presently quote) at that time appearing as a serial in *The Atlantic Monthly*.

What makes me think that the *Esquire* article had nothing to do with this sudden blow-up of wrath is that the only words quoted from it in *Late Harvest* are a reference to Norman's "loyalty and generosity to old friends". If I were making that statement now I fear I should have to make considerable qualifications, but at the risk of a digression I think I should say that when I wrote that I was thinking about his old friend, Ellingham Brooks, the English poet on Capri. I believe readers of Norman's writings will agree that he shows an uncommon severity of judgment on most contemporary poets without giving more than a hint or two that he cared much for poetry at all. His one book on the subject occupies itself, significantly, not with the poetry but the natural history of the *Greek Anthology*. When Norman (instead of giving his own prose versions, which would have been first-rate) decided that he must have verse renderings from the *Anthology*, he called upon Ellingham Brooks, although by that time Norman was famous enough to have received willing aid from any of the

scholar-poets of the time. I am thinking, for example, of
Mr. F. L. Lucas, who has made such remarkably fine verse
translations from the *Greek Anthology*. Let me give one or
two specimens of Mr. Brooks's verse as printed in *Birds
and Beasts of the Greek Anthology*. Here is one about a
hedgehog by an anonymous writer:

> "This hedgehog bristling with its pointed spines,
> Gatherer of grapes and spoiler of the vines,
> Having caught rolled like a ball his grapes among,
> Comalus has alive here up to Bacchus hung."

Read it carefully, savour it, and then enjoy this
sepulchral inscription in the English of Norman's friend:

> "Too soon, Phænocritus, desired by all
> Who sojourn in Ialysus, did'st fall
> In Lethe's sea, after gleaning so brief
> In lettered lore, and o'er thy tomb their grief
> Showed even the owls that never weep. Again
> No voice of singer hereafter will greet
> The generations yet to come with strain
> As sweet as thine, while men walk on their feet."

And here is just one more, memorable from the fact
that Norman specifically says he prefers this rendering to
Cowper's:

"Child of Athens, honey-nurtured, wouldst thou for thy
  feathered brood
A prattling cicada capture, feasting them upon such food?
Shall garrulous on garrulous, winged on the wingéd prey,
And shall the guest of summer-time be summer-guests'
  purvey?

Wil'st thou not drop it instantly? Neither just nor meet
　　this wrong
That singer's mouth should swallow up another skilled in
　　song."

It so happened that just before I wrote that *Esquire*
article I came across a number of copies of *Birds and Beasts
of the Greek Anthology* remaindered at twenty-five cents in a
drugstore, and bought one or two as an act of piety. Re-
reading the book with more attention to the translations I
could not help marvelling that Norman, with his austerely
high standards of poetic excellence, should have used this
clumsy doggerel, especially since, as I say, any poet of
the time would have been glad to help him. At last I saw
what it was. The translations were a tribute not to Poetry
but to Friendship. Brooks, I said to myself, was poor and
ageing and had not been able to get any of his work
published (except a sonnet in Trower's guide-book) and
then along comes Norman with splendid generosity and in
the spirit of auld lang syne includes Brooks's travesties of
the *Anthology* in his own incomparable prose. It was that
which drew my willing tribute to his "loyalty and
generosity to old friends", and nothing whatever in his
treatment of Magnus.

I must now bore the reader with the text of mine which
I find cited in *Late Harvest*, although to the best of my
recollection it appeared originally in *The Atlantic Monthly*
and not in *Esquire*:

　　"Curiously enough, the most realistic (though satirical)
　　portrait of Norman Douglas is the Argyle of Lawrence's
　　novel, *Aaron's Rod*. This was the real cause of the breach
　　between those two and of Norman's anti-Lawrence
　　pamphlet, though the ostensible *casus belli* was

Lawrence's superbly written introduction to the
memoirs of Maurice Magnus, who served in the French
Foreign Legion and eventually committed suicide in
Malta.

"It is not for me to judge my two friends in this unhappy controversy. Lawrence was not always master of
his pen when moved by resentment, and I think it very
probable that Norman was right when he said Lawrence
misjudged and misrepresented the unhappy Magnus. On
the other hand, Norman obviously resented the too
vivid and unflattering portrait of himself in *Aaron's Rod*,
and his charge that Lawrence acted meanly is absurd.
At the time Lawrence was poor, his income uncertain,
and he had a wife. Magnus lived with an extravagance
which to the frugal Lawrence was an outrage, and he was
unmarried. Why on earth should Lawrence have given
more than half the small sum he had in the world to a
comparative stranger who, he had every reason to
think, was a waster and perhaps a crook? Norman had
much more money than Lawrence, and Magnus was his
friend, not Lawrence's. Why didn't he lend Magnus
the money for lack of which the wretched man killed
himself? Moreover, it is no credit to Norman that he
accepted a gift of a hundred pounds to write the
pamphlet, from a wealthy person who had a grudge
against Lawrence. And after doing that, Norman had
the crust to abuse Lawrence for not being a gentleman!"

There is a correction to make in that. Magnus asked
for £35 to £40, and Lawrence said he possessed only
£60. Possibly that was all he had in Italy, but a diary of
jottings shows that his total fortune at the time was
£171. He paid Magnus's hotel bills and gave him money
to get out of Italy. Magnus went first-class to Malta while

the Lawrences, who were on the same boat, had to go second! In view of Norman's post-mortem tribute to Magnus (whom, however, he had referred to previously in *Alone*), it is perhaps worth recollecting Frieda Lawrence's views on this situation. This is what she wrote:

"Later Magnus appeared at our Fontana Vecchia at Taormina having fled from Montecassino. He came almost taking for granted that we would be responsible for him, that it was our duty to keep him. This disturbed Lawrence.

" 'Is it my duty to look after this man?' he asked me.

"To me it was no problem. Had I been fond of Magnus, had he had any meaning, or purpose, but no, he seemed only antisocial, a poor devil without any pride, and he didn't seem to matter anyhow. With the money Lawrence lent him, he stayed at the best hotel in Taormina, to my great resentment, we who could not afford to stay even in a second rate hotel. I felt he made a fool of Lawrence, and afterwards, when we went to Malta, crossing second class from Palermo, whom should I discover gaily swanking and talking to an English Navy officer but Magnus on the first-class deck! The cheek of the man!"

I cannot feel that in *Late Harvest* Norman made any effective answer to my two paragraphs, and of course he never attempted to answer Frieda's remarks. Norman denies that he was annoyed by *Aaron's Rod*, but he had evidently forgotten that this is at variance with what he had himself written. He cannot claim that he gave money to Magnus in Sicily or Malta, for if he had Magnus could have escaped to Egypt, but tries to trail a red herring by quoting my remarks about his generosity and loyalty to old

friends. He does not deny the subsidy business, and merely
trails another red herring. Finally he writes a long paragraph of abuse of a harmless sort, though not so intended,
in which he implies that Lawrence (and I suppose I too) is
denounced for writing what would be "bad form in a
community of stable-boys and scullery-maids". *O altitudo*!

My share in all this is that of the usual well-meaning
third party. When I wrote that, I had no intention whatever of annoying the old gentleman. I said a lot in praise of
him and his books, hoping he might be pleased as he had
been before, and that I might even sell a few copies of his
works; but I saw no reason why I should not express
myself frankly on this Lawrence-Magnus affair. My
mistake was in thinking that the reconciliation between
them had been sincere and in underestimating Douglas's
resentment and indeed hatred of Lawrence. I believed
what I had been told in Florence—that there had been a
falling out of old friends and then a reconciliation staged by
Pino, with mutual forgiving and forgetting. This may have
been sincere on Lawrence's part, but not on the part of
Norman, who continued to sell his pamphlet and to maintain a grudge. I should, of course, have taken warning
from what he says of Lawrence in *Looking Back*, but I
assumed he was putting down his version of Lawrence 'for
the record', as they say, and two items attracted my
attention. One was Norman's admirable little vignette of
his scattering red carnations on Lawrence's grave, 'an
inoffensive gesture' which seemed the quiet end of all
contention. The other was the ignorance of Lawrence's
work showed by his printing Lawrence's poem 'Green' (as
if it were something unpublished!) whereas it had already
appeared in one of the *Imagist Anthologies*, in *Look! We
Have Come Through*, and in *Collected Poems*.

It seemed that Norman's hatred for Lawrence, far from

being appeased, grew with the passage of time, especially since he found that Lawrence's writings, far from disappearing as he expected, stood much higher in general esteem than his own. In *Late Harvest* he speaks of Lawrence's "cat-like disposition", says that "nothing was sacred" to him, says he stabbed one in the back, wrote stories which were 'scurrilous' and 'libellous' and wound up with that line about 'stable-boys'—a dangerous reference which exposed him to a very sharp retort.

Apropos that subsidy affair, Norman asks: "Can anyone else divulge the origin of this legend?" Premising that I don't think it a legend, I can—it came spontaneously from the man who knew Douglas best—from Pino Orioli. Now, of course, Pino was a fantasist who wove many a wild story. Moreover, he had not a strict regard for truth. But no man can be always lying and for sheer lack of invention Pino frequently deviated into truth. With time one came to see which stories were the fruit of imagination, which an improvement of fact and which were true. The imaginary ones almost always had an erotic and satirical turn, and one of them suddenly occurs to me. There was a rather ugly old literary spinster Pino greatly disliked because he thought her 'si si'. One day, with much gravity, he told me a long story about how she had once been kissed by some celebrated person, though Pino failed to explain how he witnessed this. Then came the well-known gleam in his eye, as he asked me almost with solemnity:

"And do you know vhat she muss do vhen he kiss her?"

"No."

"She is so surprise a man can kiss her—she *faint*!"

Anyone who believed that story would believe anything, but however much Pino may be discounted as a witness, what motive had he for inventing a story so completely without humour and so intrinsically probable as the pamphlet subsidy, especially as Pino seemed to think it was A Good Thing? What made me take notice was that I had heard somehow—I think from Norman himself, but I am not sure—that when writing the Magnus pamphlet he had stayed in the best hotel at Syracuse in Sicily. Why and how? Not so long before he had been in desperate straits in Paris and Mentone, scarcely knowing where his next meal was to be had. This Syracuse hotel had been spoken of so often that he could not deny it, and accordingly we find his stay at this expensive hotel excused in *Late Harvest* because, he says, he found "good food and attentive service essential" for him to produce "serious work". What nonsense! Compared with his real books, the Magnus pamphlet is a mere piece of spiteful journalism which he could have written in a café or in his bath. The hollowness of this claim about good food and attentive service being 'essential' to his best writing is unguardedly exposed by himself in the same book. On page forty-eight he tells us that a great part of *Old Calabria* was written during a "spell of acute financial depression" in dingy lodgings at King's Cross, Chiswick Lane and Kew! And on page seventy-four, *Siren Land*, he says, was written in an empty, abandoned and supposedly haunted cottage near Sorrento with one peasant boy in attendance! Norman had too much Scottish good sense and thrift to stay at a place like that expensive Syracuse hotel unless his expenses were paid. And if they were paid, why not credit the rest of Pino's story that Norman also received a Poet Laureate's *douceur* for the heightening of his vein? If on the other hand we accept the incredible story that Norman paid for himself at the hotel and received no subsidy, then it seems rather regrettable and out of keeping with the

N

immense regard he professes for Magnus that he should have spent on luxurious living the money which might have saved Magnus from his death.

"He? He is tagging your epitaph."

It is strange what an Até of discord Lawrence was in his generation, and what an amount of bickering and bad ink he managed to breed. Norman is far indeed from being the only person who to the end of his days burned with vindictive hate for the wandering consumptive genius. The recent remarks of certain eminent persons over the B.B.C. are a case in point—who would have thought the old men had so much hate in them? Is there an explanation? I think there is, and to begin it I have to ask Mr. David Garnett's permission to quote again some remarks of his which go to the root of the problem:

> "Lawrence was a natural copy-cat; indeed, he was the only great mimic I have ever known; he had a genius for 'taking people off', and could reproduce voice and manner exactly."

(He could, and let me add that he had the much rarer gift of being able to "reproduce voice and manner exactly" in his novels.)

> "The slightest affectation of manner or social pretence was seized on mercilessly. One realised the enormous æsthetic enjoyment which the poor are afforded by the spectacle of the imbecilities of the rich, of the endless 'copy' they provide."

And on another page of the same essay Mr. Garnett sums it up in a sentence when he writes of Lawrence:

> "He was the type who provokes the most violent

class-hatred in this country: the impotent hatred of the
upper classes for the lower."

Naturally a man with a personal and literary gift like
this, who uses it freely and without any regard for persons,
will not be popular with his victims. At the same time the
mimicry was æsthetic as well as spiteful, since, as Mr.
Garnett truly says, "the person whom Lawrence most
constantly made fun of was himself," and "he mimicked
himself ruthlessly and continuously." This is exactly what
the people he 'satirised' never did—they were far too
pompous and thought far too much of themselves. Nor
did they ever acknowledge Lawrence's self-satire.
Lawrence had this exceptionally clear-sighted perception
of what he and others intrinsically and really were, and a
derisive skill in tearing down the pomps and pretences and
poses with which they deceived themselves as well as
others. In Norman's world everyone had a 'gentlemanly'
pose and in a 'gentlemanly' way accepted the poses of the
others. They were all clad in the Emperor's imaginary
robes of superiority, and along comes Lawrence with his
wicked titter, saying: "Look! They haven't got any
clothes on, they're only pretending!" It was this which so
much infuriated Douglas and other gentlemanly persons
and writers, and their rage was redoubled by the fact that
this 'cheek' came from a working man and that they lacked
the gifts to retaliate on him in kind. Norman tried hard,
but all his attempts at satirising Lawrence lack Lawrence's
vivid realism and gift of laughter. Although a minor victim
(let off very lightly) in *Aaron's Rod*, I can never read the
book without laughing aloud at the perfection with which
Lawrence has hit off his various unconscious portrait-
sitters.

It seems to me that Norman was very sensitive about

being 'put into' novels as a character, and saw it as an
affront to his dignity, though, as I shall show later on, he
had not the least hesitation about writing caricatures of
then living people himself. As a matter of fact I think
most people do feel insulted if they have been at all
caricatured in print, though it is supposed to be an honour
if drawn in black and white. I had a curious example of
this myself. Whenever I published anything I had a copy
sent to Norman, not that I expected him to read it (why on
earth should he?) but simply as a mark of respect, and he
knew I did not even want him to bother to acknowledge
receipt. In 1933 a novel was sent him, and some time later
I was puzzled by receiving a rather stiff reply to a letter of
mine and words to the effect that he had read my book as
far as page sixty-eight. I got the impression that on this
page sixty-eight I must have said something to offend him,
so I looked it up, and found it to be the last of three pages
dealing with a character I called Scrope—which name I
took from Shakespeare, not knowing then that it was also
the name of a celebrated mineralogist favourably mentioned
in one of Norman's books. This character belonged to an
old family, had been close to but not (so far as I remember
the book) actually a member of the diplomatic service, had
travelled, had written books, and used to criticise the
government after dinner. He was represented not at all
satirically as an impressive elderly man with ideas of his
own. It dawned on me that Norman thought I was
sketching him, but as a matter of fact I had never thought
of him, and the character (though considerably altered)
had been suggested by Wilfrid Blunt, whom I had met
pre-1914 through Yeats and Ezra Pound. On reflection I
thought perhaps Norman might have been more offended if
I told him the truth than if I said nothing, so I said nothing.
But, if I didn't misinterpret him, that oblique hint was

rather characteristic. He enjoyed these diplomatic subtleties and *astuces*. Of course if he had looked into another book published some years later I don't say but what he might have found something nearer home.

Lawrence's account of Norman by name in his Magnus introduction and the livelier portrait of him as James Argyle in *Aaron's Rod* both dated back to experiences at the end of 1919, and must have been written down within a year or two. But similar scenes were still going on in the early 1930s, and the talk and characteristics of Argyle are of a most authentic reality:

"The party that evening consisted all of men: Francis and Angus, and a writer, James Argyle, and little Algy Constable and tiny Louis Mee and deaf Walter Rosen. They all snapped and rattled at one another, and were rather spiteful but rather amusing. Francis and Angus had to leave early. They had another appointment. And James Argyle got quite tipsy and said to Aaron:

" 'But, my boy, don't let yourself be led astray by the talk of such people as Algy. Beware of them, my boy, if you've a soul to save. If you've a soul to save!' And he swallowed the remains of his litre.

"Algy's nose trembled a little, and his eyes blinked.

" 'And if you've a soul to *lose*,' he said, 'I would warn you very earnestly against Argyle.' Whereupon Algy shut one eye and opened the other so wide, that Aaron was almost scared.

" 'Quite right, my boy! Ha! Ha! Never a truer thing said. Ha-Ha-Ha.' Argyle laughed his Mephistophelian tipsy laugh. 'They'll teach you to save. Never was such a lot of ripe old savers! Save their old trouser buttons! Ha-ha! What's a soul, to them——?'

" 'What is it to you, is perhaps the more pertinent question,' said Algy, flapping his eyelids like some crazy owl. 'It is you who specialise in the matter of soul, and we who are in need of enlightenment——'

" 'Yes, very true, you *are*. You *are* in need of enlightenment. A set of benighted wise virgins. Ha-ha-ha! That's good that—benighted wise virgins. What—' Argyle put his red face near to Aaron's, and made a *moue** narrowing his eyes quizzically as he peered up from under his level grey eye-brows. 'Sit in the dark to save the lamp-oil! And all no good to them. When the bridegroom cometh——! Ha-ha! Good that! Good, my boy! The bridegroom——' he giggled to himself. 'What about the bridegroom, Algy, my boy? Eh? What about him? Better trim your wick, old man, if it's not too late——'

" 'We were talking of souls, not wicks, Argyle,' said Algy.

" 'Same thing. Upon my soul it all amounts to the same thing. Where's the soul in a man that hasn't got a bed-fellow—eh?—answer me that! Can't be done, you know. Might as well ask a virgin chicken to lay you an egg. But, believe me, there's far more damned chastity in the world, than anything else. Even in this town. Call it chastity, if you like. I see nothing in it but sterility. It takes a rat to praise long tails. Impotence set up the praise of it. The virtue is made out of the necessity. Ha-ha-ha! They can't do it, and so they make a virtue of not doing it. Like them! Like them!' "

There now comes a pause in the talk—"Argyle was in his cups, which left no more to be said." The party starts breaking up, with some discussion about Aaron's playing

* For a photograph of this *moue* see page 154 of Orioli's *Moving Along.*

his flute (gratis) at Algy's, and Argyle strenuously urging him not to, but to make them all buy tickets for his concert. As Algy leaves, Argyle has another smack at him, and then he and Aaron (Lawrence) are left alone:

". . . Argyle arched his brows at Aaron, saying:

" 'Oh, my dear fellow, what a lot they are! Little Mee—looking like an innocent little boy. He's over seventy if he's a day. Well over seventy. Well, you don't believe me. Ask his mother—ask his mother. She's ninety-five. Old lady of ninety-five——' Argyle laughed himself at his own preposterousness.

" 'And then Algy—Algy's not a fool, you know. Oh, he can be most entertaining, most witty, and amusing. But he's out of place here. He should be in Kensington; dandling round the ladies' drawing-rooms and making his *mots*. They're rich, you know, the pair of them. Little Mee used to boast that he lived on eleven-and-threepence a week. Had to, poor chap. But then what does a white mouse like that need? Makes a heavy meal on a cheese-paring. Luck, you know—but, of course, he's come into money as well. Rich as Croesus, and still lives on nineteen-and-twopence a week. Though it's nearly double, of course, what it used to be. No wonder he looks anxious. They disapprove of me—oh, quite right, quite right from their point of view. Where would their money be otherwise? It wouldn't last long if I laid hands on it——' he made a devilish quizzing face. 'But you know, they get on my nerves. Little old maids, you know, little old maids. I'm sure I'm surprised at their patience with me. But when people are patient with you, you want to spit gall at them. Don't you? Ha-ha-ha! Poor old Algy. Did I lay it on him, to-night, or did I miss him?'

" 'I think you got him,' said Aaron.

" 'He'll never forgive me. Depend on it, he'll never forgive me. Ha-ha! I like to be unforgiven. It adds *zest* to one's intercourse with people, to know that they'll never forgive one. Ha-ha-ha! Little old maids, who do their knitting with their tongues. Poor old Algy—he drops his stitches now. Ha-ha-ha! Must be eighty, I should say.' "

This is part of the portrait of himself which Norman pretended to brush off as 'playful caricature'. There is laughter in it, but the laughter is about as 'playful' as a jaguar which has just caught a peccary. As to 'caricature' —no doubt the portrait is satiric, but the satire is that of merciless verity, not of exaggeration. And as the portrait is developed in later scenes, it shows Argyle in other aspects—as a courteous host, for instance, and as a cynical thinker in the discussions on socialism and slavery and on women and marriage. I can't see that Lawrence is unfair in his treatment of 'Argyle', still less that he is in any sense abusive or that he attributes to 'Argyle' any untrue or unfair trait,* anything in short which was not in the original. Along with that extraordinary gift of 'mimicry' there went that equally extraordinary ability to see through upper-class and 'gentlemanly' pretence. Lawrence refuses to take Douglas at his own valuation. By the time Lawrence had done with him there did not remain one rag of the Wardour Street duniwassal. And the same is true of even his physical appearance:

"He must have been very handsome in his day, with his natural dignity, and his clean-shaven strong square face. But now his face was all red and softened and

* Which Norman certainly did to at least two characters in *South Wind*.

inflamed, his eyes had gone small and wicked under his bushy grey brows. Still he had a presence. And his grey hair, almost gone white, was still handsome."

Pitiless, but, in my experience, entirely true.

In *Late Harvest* Norman tells us that this 'playful caricature' was not the reason for his 'taking up arms' against Lawrence, had nothing to do with it. When Norman came to write his Magnus diatribe *Aaron's Rod* was 'ancient history'. Well, it wasn't so ancient that he had forgotten it, for he spends two pages of the pamphlet in denouncing the *Aaron's Rod* portrait of "me, under the transparent disguise of Jimmie McTaggart or something equally Scotch," and making dignified protests that he had *not* accused his Florentine bachelor friends of being mean. Nearly ten years later he again brought up *Aaron's Rod* in *Looking Back* (p. 346), quoting two pages of a rambling offended letter from the 'Sir William' who is a character in the novel. This letter is dated February, 1925, and shows that even after the publication of the Magnus pamphlet, to 'defend the memory of his injured friend,' Norman was trying to use the annoyance created by *Aaron's Rod* against its author. If it was such 'ancient history' why keep bringing it up? 'Sir William', by the way, put Lawrence up for a couple of nights in Italy (for which he was overpaid with copies of *Twilight in Italy* and *Sons and Lovers*), on the strength of which Norman condescendingly places him among Lawrence's 'protectors'! What feudal dignity! I think I know what Lawrence would have said of such protectors—chest protectors—*couvre-toi de gloire, Tartarin,* * *couvre-toi de flanelle!*

No, I still think that with so vain a man 'James Argyle' rankled, as did the companion sketch in Lawrence's M.M.

* Or "Tartuffe"?

Introduction, for which Douglas had specifically given him permission by letter to "put me in too if you like." Here again there is merciless verity of observation from the "disreputable little hat" to the Scottish thrift of refusing to pay for a little wine left in the bottom of a flask. Norman tries to throw this off—he can't deny it—by saying that if there is wine left in a flask and you don't get it weighed and the money repaid, Italians think you are not quite right in the head. Well, yes, if there is a litre or more remaining, but if there is less you leave it as part of the waiter's tip, the over-worked waiter whom Lawrence shows Norman treating so 'callously' by sitting on and on after everyone else had gone and the servitor was collapsing with fatigue and malaria.

Now this Scottish 'thrift' must have been evident to everybody who knew Norman (though it may have gone with moods of extravagance), which raises the problem of why it was that Norman so often denounced other people for meanness. It became almost a minor obsession, and Lawrence has faithfully reproduced one of Norman's whimsical diatribes against what he called the 'meanness' of those people in Florence. I can't accept Norman's denial, for I have myself heard him give off just such amusing denunciations, and against those very people.

Complaints of meanness in his friends may be found in *Looking Back*. Turn to the remarks on Mr. Alfred Grote (wrong name), who is said to have had £5,000 a year and had often given Norman "food for thought" by making him wish that "some competent person would write a study on"—what do you suppose?—'meanness', "the recent growth of meanness". And he goes on to attribute this deplorable state of affairs to the increase of male homosexuals, suppressed and otherwise, who, he says, are "more close-fisted than heterosexuals" and "spend absurdly small sums on clothes and amusements." Far be it from me to contradict such an authority, but I should say that meanness is one trait from which male homosexuals are conspicuously free, and that they tend to over-dress and to crave expensive amusements. But perhaps this was not the case with the elderly Florentine lodge. Quite forgetting his denial that he had said anything of the sort as so faithfully recorded in *Aaron's Rod*, Norman winds up:

"It is the luncheon hour at this moment, and I prophesy that he will contrive to spend about 2s. 9d. on that meal, and be furious with you for spending more."

Compare that with the 'living on eleven and threepence a week' of *Aaron's Rod*! It is undeniably the same person talking in the one and writing in the other. And this humorous outburst against 'Grote' is not the only complaint of meanness in *Looking Back*. Whole categories of people, according to Norman, were acquiring this uncompanionable vice. "Why," he asks rhetorically, "are Anglo-Indians so infernally mean?" Well, are they? Norman thought meanness "quite a characteristic trait of that class". I'm no judge, for the only Anglo-Indians I have known personally were fellows home on leave spending two years pay in six months, and otherwise characters in history or fiction such as Warren Hastings and Colonel Newcome. It seems Norman was always running in to mean persons. There was 'Grote', and there was 'Plunkett' (a very thin disguise for Herbert Trench), who were both 'mean'. Dr. F. W. Mann, who made verse translations a little better but not much than Ellingham Brooks's, was mean because he took Norman to a cheap restaurant after talking of expensive ones. And we are also told that Lawrence was mean. It is alleged that he grudged

having "to pay for several whiskies for Orioli and myself".
This is followed by a ridiculous story about a sole, filling
two pages. All I can say is that if Lawrence really succeeded
in making Norman pay for that fish I take off my hat to him
for a hitherto unsuspected shrewdness and craft.

Pino's *Memoirs of a Bookseller* give us further instances
of Lawrence's meanness in paragraphs so obviously by
Norman and in his style that to prove the writing was his
would be superfluous. Now where did Pino (via Norman)
find Lawrence mean? Well, he received only ten per cent
of the net profits of *Lady Chatterley's Lover*, and grumbles
that it is usually the author who gets only ten per cent and
the publisher gets the remainder. What were the
conditions and terms, I wonder, on which Norman
published his books with Pino? I always understood they
each paid half the expense and took half the net profits?
Besides, a writer so comparatively successful as Lawrence
was in 1928 received not ten per cent, but twenty per cent
or even twenty-five per cent of the gross takings. Moreover, in the case of *Lady C.*, Pino risked no capital as a
commercial publisher does. It was Lawrence who risked
the capital and paid all expenses, Pino acting merely as
distributor, for which not very arduous feat £160 was
not bad pay. Does not this show how difficult it was for
Norman to find anything of which he could accuse
Lawrence when he has to cook up such absurd stories?

Here is another typical Douglas-in-an-Orioli's-skin
attempt to be venomous at Lawrence's expense:

"He lived . . . at the Villa Mirenda, a distant and
dilapidated place among the hills with no water supply
and only one small fire-place. . . . There was a
peasant family near at hand and on one occasion he gave
them a Christmas tree, with carol-singing on his part,

and presents for the two or three little children costing
forty-eight centimes apiece."

Now here is a bitchy suggestion of miserly discomfort
and Chadbandish charity and the whole thing is a lie.
The Villa Mirenda was a large Tuscan farm-house of which
the Lawrences had the whole upper floor—it is the large
building in the background of the photograph labelled
'Villa Mirenda' reproduced in Lawrence's *Letters*. As I
stayed in the Villa myself I can say definitely it was larger,
healthier and infinitely more peaceful than Douglas's flat
over that 'crash-box' of Lungarno delle Grazie. The beds
at the Mirenda were hard, the furnishing simple, but it
was not dilapidated. I never noticed any lack of water, and
I am pretty sure there was running water in the kitchen.
There were fine views of the distant Duomo from the
look-out. One fireplace! I don't remember how many
there were, there may have been only one, but can you
imagine a coal-miner's son allowing himself to be cold if
fuel was available, and there was plenty up there? Whenever I saw him in winter Lawrence always had a good fire, if
it was only of furze roots, and sat hunched close up to it, as
his father had done, and loved the warmth. Why would he
want to sit by two fires, anyway?

And then that sneer about the peasants and the Christmas tree! Now, if Pino really wrote that paragraph
(which I don't believe) he showed a deplorable lack of
memory, for he published the first edition of the book
which contained the complete refutation of what is said.
I should think it highly likely that Douglas, with his well-
developed hate of Lawrence, never even looked at it. If
he had, he would have been more careful and not have left
Pinorman so completely open to conviction for falsehood.
The book to which I refer is *Young Lorenzo*, in which

Lawrence's sister published a letter, written a few days before the first of these parties, in which the preparations are told in detail. Moreover, Frieda's book and another letter of Lawrence's prove there were two of these parties, not one, as Pinorman asserts. To the first there were invited not just one family and 'two or three little children', but twenty-seven persons belonging to several families, of whom fifteen were adults and twelve were children. Next Christmas there was another tree, and seventeen persons were present. Now here is the truth to refute that lie:

"We are busy getting ready a Christmas tree for our peasants. There will be about twelve children, and I expect their parents will have to come to look. So many people work on this little estate. And the children are wild little things. They've never seen a Christmas tree, but they heard of some other English people who made one for the peasants, so they all had fits hoping we'd do one. We got all sorts of little wooden toys from Florence, and with a few glittering things and some sweets and dates, and the candles, it'll do for them. They never get sweets or anything like that from year's end to year's end. They're much poorer than even the really poor in England . . . But we've no idea how poorly they really live—like cattle. Still they are nice, and when we give them things, they always send us back a few dried grapes, or figs, or olives.

"We shall give them their Christmas tree on Friday evening at sundown. And if the twenty-seven all of them come, it'll be like Ripley fair in this salotta. The men will have to have a glass of sweet wine, and a long cigar called a Toscana, and the women get a glass of wine and a few biscuits. There will be a buzz!"

I am not aware that Lawrence ever claimed any kudos
for this and the next year's Christmas trees, which are
only recorded for 1926 in the letter to his sister and for
1927 in a letter to Dorothy Brett. Certainly he and
Frieda bought the little toys and tree decorations at the
Quarant'Otto (Woolworth's) in Florence. Were they
supposed to buy presents from Fortnum and Mason's and
the Rue de la Paix? And what a snobbish sneer is that
'forty-eight centimes'? A gentleman, one would suppose,
would measure an act of kindness by its intention, the
goodwill and trouble given to it, and not by the number of
centimes paid for a child's toy. And is it permitted to ask
what has been recorded that Norman Douglas ever did for
poor Italians except to wheedle them out of their wine and
try to pervert their children? I dare say these entertain-
ments did not cost more than a pound or two, but they
cost time and trouble and kindness; and, just as in the
Magnus episode, Lawrence spent and gave something,
while Douglas did nothing at the time, and afterwards
sneered.

"These people were not very happy with Lawrence,
because they expected to make a little money out of him
with washing and so forth, and never did."

If Pino really wrote that, which I don't believe, I do not
ever talk with him again, be it in heaven or be it in hell. Of
course, Frieda always did the washing, it was her *métier*,
her box at the opera—she did it wonderfully and loved
doing it, as only a baron's daughter could love such an
occupation. But I know she bought vegetables and
chickens and so forth from the *contadini*, because I was
with her when she did so. I even remember her saying:
"*Lo dirai alla Giulia*" when something was proposed
(evidently because we, her guests, were there) which she
feared 'Lorenzo' might think extravagant, and so wanted

to ask him first. That Giulia helped with the house work, and was paid for it—and there wasn't any weighing of the last glass of Chianti in the flask.

The reader will be interested to learn that Lawrence's psychology gave Norman 'food for thought'. And after chewing it over he came to the conclusion that Lawrence was "certainly one of the most envy-bitten mortals" he (Norman) had ever known. All I say to that is that I wish Norman Douglas had been brought up as one of five children in a home where the total housekeeping money very seldom exceeded thirty-five shillings a week. Norman has recorded a single meal on which he spent seventeen pounds. The undoubted fact that Lawrence, a poor man, in youth tried to spare his mother, and, as a married man, his wife, the unending chores of house-work, is attributed by Norman to 'a masochistic strain'. In the homes of manual labourers there are no scullery-maids or house-maids or stable-boys; and Lawrence, a poor man, did for his wife what he had done for his mother.

It is a mere verbal point—and so not worth making— that one page after accusing Lawrence of 'envy' Norman, on the wrong side of his mouth, praises him for having (my italics): "an *enviable* flair, an *enviable* freshness, an *enviable* mastery." I let it go at that. Of course, Norman did not approve Lawrence's writing without making serious reserves. He thought that page after page of the dialogue in *Women in Love* was 'drivel', the 'chatter of third-rate people'. Well, it is true that Lawrence's dialogue, in its truth to the speech of common people, does sometimes run to triviality, and sometimes goes on too long. But in his dialogue I almost always hear a human voice speaking. Talking of drivel, I wonder what Lawrence would have said of a piece of amateurish and stilted dialogue like this

from *They Went*. I wish I could have heard him, I do wish
it.

" 'This is what I wished you to see, children,' said
Manthis. 'Unicorns are lonely things and notoriously
scarce. Now you know the reason why. They have no
sense of family life; they never take care of their offspring. They forget their parents, their children; their
wives and their husbands. They only think of those
wonderful horns. Look at him!'

" 'How truly pitiful,' observed the babchick.

" 'We are the lonely unicorns, Princess,' said a voice
at that young person's side.

It was Theophilus again.

" 'Tell me, Theophilus—tell me about those dragon's
scales, and how we may be able to copy them out of
such metal as the town contains. I would gladly learn
your process and if it be a secret, I will pay what price
you ask. Our old sorcerer, Lelian——'

" 'Let us talk about it, Princess, on some other occasion.
I must, alas, leave you this very moment, having given
my word to certain friends to meet them within an
hour.' " (Norman Douglas; *They Went*, p. 120.)

"I trust I am not violent"—but I should be interested to
learn of any passage of Lawrence's novels which is comparable with that for stilted 'drivel' if we must use such
scurrilous terms as 'drivel'. In Lawrence's dialogue, even
at its most ordinary, the reader feels that genuine human
voices are speaking, individual voices, whereas Norman
seldom indeed achieves this, and his dialogue is nearly
always 'literary'. However good it is—and it is sometimes very good indeed—the real speaker is always
Norman, and his characters almost all share his prejudices,

his points of views, and even his mannerisms of language. He couldn't even edit Pino without making him talk like Norman Douglas, as it was said by Goldsmith that Dr. Johnson would make little fishes talk like great whales.

The most irrational aspect of Norman's feud with Lawrence has yet to be mentioned—a rather vindictive follow-up of the sordid Magnus affair. I don't think I am unfair in saying Norman was vindictive (and I certainly don't imagine that other people, including Lawrence, are not vindictive), but the following passage about a school-master he had hated seems rather vehement:

"Such was my loathing for this worm in human form, and such is still my existing rancour against him, that if somebody were to assure me officially that he had died of a lingering and painful disease I should rejoice from the bottom of my heart." (*Looking Back*, p. 480.)

Making all allowances for a verve which sometimes ran away with him and for that vein of *Simplicissimus* caricature and whimsicality, I can't help feeling that the emotion expressed and the vindictive grudge against this wretched pedant are a little excessive after fifty years. In his vindictiveness against Lawrence, which was as bitter in 1950 as it was in 1923, Norman was led into taking up the preposterous attitude that while it was perfectly legitimate for him and his friend Compton Mackenzie to satirise their ex-friends and acquaintances in their novels, it was blackguardly, ungentlemanly and caddish for Lawrence to do exactly the same thing, even though he did it much better. This is an interesting survival of the *ancien régime*— one law for the gentleman and another for the serf.

If Norman had not given me the information in the pages of *Looking Back*, I should not have known that some of the characters in *Vestal Fires* and *Extraordinary Women* are portraits of then living persons—a practice of his friend which Norman whole-heartedly approves. So much so that he adopted it himself. From the 1946 preface to *South Wind* we learn, with Norman's full concurrence, that the portraits of Freddy Parker and his 'lady' were intended for the British Consular Agent and author of the *Book of Capri* and his wife, Mr. and Mrs. Harold Trower:

> ". . . a particularly objectionable pair of English residents, both dead now. I did what I could for them and they, at least, could have been recognised from my sketch, as I meant them to be."

Surely that is a complete give-away? Lawrence's 'ungentlemanly' conduct consisted in his writing about Magnus and Norman by name and with Norman's permission, and about Norman and various other people, friends of his, in a manner which Norman disliked because it made him and them look ridiculous—which is exactly what he admits he did, and vindictively, to Mr. and Mrs. Trower. What was sauce in the Eastwood goose, however, was highly gentlemanly feeling in the Tilquhillie gander. Sample a few of the highly gentlemanly epithets Norman gratuitously fastened on Trower (in his life-time) with the hope that his victim would be recognised:

> "Stumpy and pompous-looking; flushed in the face . . . with shifty grey eyes . . . an incomparable ass . . . a fool . . . a really remarkable combination of malevolence and imbecility . . . stolid pachydermous obliquity . . . the worst kind of Englishman . . . but for the wise counsels of his lady he would have been in the lock-up over and over again . . . his whole

o*

existence was a tangle of shady and ignoble transactions
. . . a retail welsher . . ."

I believe you might comb all Lawrence's voluminous
writings without being able to discover any parallel to this
kind of thing, simply because he was too good an artist to
drop into the stereotyped abuse of a foul-mouthed schoolboy in a rage, and because when he wanted to be offensive
he knew that nothing was more deadly than undeniable
facts—as witness Argyle in his cups. These elegant
flowers of rhetoric dropped on Trower point up one of
Norman's fine-old-Scottish-gentleman pronouncements on
literature, which I think he silently borrowed from
Hazlitt:

> "Portraiture of character and events should take the
> form of one gentleman conversing with another, in the
> easy tone of good society,"

such as "You incomparable ass!", "You retail welsher!",
"You fool!" and so forth.

I have just re-read the whole of the Argyle parts of
Aaron's Rod and the short story, *Two Blue Birds*, which
Norman describes as "scurrilous and libellous". Although
they are most effective satirically there is not a single
merely abusive phrase to be found in them. Lawrence was,
for one thing, too clever to give these high-born gentles
a legitimate chance to put their tongues out at him with
"Yah, blinking charity kid, can't write like a gentleman!"
The effect of disdain and contempt in Lawrence's short
story is most subtly obtained by an ironic politeness and
smoothness of phrase and a seemingly perfect fairness.
When you compare the men's writings, the effect is that of
the sooty old pot on the Victorian coal fire gurgling 'Black

as Tartarus!' to the polished aluminium kettle on the electric stove. 'Scurrilous' Norman calls this story, but according to the *Oxford Dictionary* the word 'scurrilous' means:

"Using such language as only the license of a buffoon can justify (Johnson); characterised by coarseness of language."

'Scurrilous', then, is not the word to apply to a finely-written, restrained and suave satire such as *Two Blue Birds*, but to the kind of writer who calls people retail welshers and asses, and describes the admirers of a better writer than himself as 'stable-boys and scullery-maids' because he can think of nothing more cogent to say in depreciation.

Another character in *South Wind* who is treated in what the dictionary defines as a 'scurrilous' manner is the judge, Malipizzo. Among other malpractices he is depicted as selling justice for bribes, and manufacturing evidence to hang an innocent half-witted boy for murder, because the boy is a Catholic and the judge a Free-thinker. This personage, we learn from the 1946 *South Wind*, was intended for a friend of Trower's, the Capri magistrate, Capolazzi, described by Norman in his gentlemanly and easy tone of good society as "a red-haired ruffian . . . who nearly had me in the lock-up once or twice; this caricature was the best I could do, by way of being square with him."

That future biographer will have no difficulty then in discovering Norman's motive for abusing Capolazzi—i.e. he very nearly had Norman in jail. But what was Trower's offence? It cannot have been merely that he was a specimen of the offensive Englishman abroad, since there used to be so many of them with their pipes and prejudices

and accents. Pondering on the fact that the Capri
magistrate nearly had Norman in the lock-up (on what
charge or charges?) it occurred to me that in the case of an
accusation against a British subject abroad there would
naturally be a communication between the native
magistrate and H.M.'s Consular representative; and I
suddenly remembered a little incident which happened to
me in the British Consulate at Florence. I had gone there
for signatures and attestations to some of the innumerable
silly documents then required before a foreigner in Italy
could buy and drive a car. I must have made some little
grumble at this excess of bureaucratic zeal to the Consul as
he stood turning over my collections of documents. He
did not take it up until he came to an application on *carta
bollata* from me to the Minister of Justice in Rome
'obsequiously' craving from him a certificate that I had
never been in prison and had a good character. "This *is*
rather absurd," said the Consul, striking the paper with his
finger. "If you were a bad hat, we should know it long
before they did."

Trower and Capolazzi . . . the situation has given me
food for thought.

9

THIS 'Ave atque Vale' has turned into something much nearer 'A Soldier's Farewell' than I intended or expected, but the logic of facts is irresistible. If you respect them they won't let you make a sow's ear out of a silk purse.

Norman Douglas was a distinguished man but no plaster saint from the Place St. Sulpice. He was a good, and in a few books a great, writer, but he had his limitations and faults like everyone else. That future biographer should pay him the compliment of trying to tell the truth— "nothing extenuate", etc.—and be frank without either flattery on the one side or unfairness on the other. Give the devil his due. It will surely be a fascinatingly difficult study for that biographer—the handsome German-Scottish 'gent' who became a scallywag bohemian without abating his claims to aristocracy in spite of the fact that on his own showing (and all honour to him for truth-telling here) he was a bum, a spunge, a cadger, a borrower, even a swindler (remember that story in *Looking Back* about swindling the tailor of fifty francs? I never respected Norman more than when I found he had the courage and honesty to tell that story against himself) and yet always retained a certain presence and dignity. And then this 'well-bred cad' (to adopt his own Walsingham House phraseology), this lady-killer, is suddenly made a pederast through a romantic incident with a Neopolitan slum boy.

He amusingly puts out a 'philosophy' of extreme hedonism with unabashed candour in an age of mealy-mouthed servitude to inferiors, when every penny-a-liner will insult a Queen or a Cardinal while abjectly flattering the ignominious mob, and yet refutes his own philosophy in the days when the cicada became a burden, by suffering a boredom and misery of blankness which made me understand for the first time that *taedium vitae* of which the Romans complained so bitterly and so eloquently. What a study; what a character to explain; what a story to tell; what a career to investigate! But devilish difficult, far too difficult for me, who must confine myself to these barren notes and fluctuating memories. And then the delicious paradox of his becoming up-to-date by being so far behind the times, of his being taken up too by the snobby *ersatz* highbrows whom he despised so heartily . . .! That will be a difficult biography.

All readers of Norman Douglas will have noticed his habit of using catch phrases of his own devising or adoption, which somehow seem to bring him back more than anything else. There was that "Cinquecento!" and the ever-ready "What next!" and that "It stands to reason that . . ." which introduced some extravagant fancy or intentional absurdity. ("It stands to reason that the Duchess was an American.") "Disheartening" was a favourite word, which he should not have introduced into books signed by Pino, who never used it and probably didn't know what it meant. There was "Poof, my dear . . .", which had a variety of meanings and uses, and the greetings, "Hello, deary," and "Hello, Chawly," and "Pinch of snuff, deary." There was "Drunk as David's sow," which, as Norman truly said, nobody can explain. (I suspect it goes back to the days when an exclusive aristocracy took every allusion to Poodle Byng and knew why they said "queer as Dick's hat-band".) A frequent one was "*Warum nicht!*", put out with that schoolboy chuckle or giggle when he was trying to urge one to some excess of wine or food. "Give the devil her due" I have mentioned before. "I'll tell you" was his inevitable response, as he pulled out his watch, if you asked the time. His most inspired phrase, which I think he uses in *How About Europe?* was: "Can cretinism go further? Of course it can!"

Like other bigoted rationalists Norman had a good many superstitions, which were supposed to be jokes, but perhaps not wholly so. He thought every seventh year of life a dangerous one, particularly when the seven was multiplied by nine (I have forgotten why) so that he was extremely relieved when he safely passed sixty-three. Then, he had local and special superstitions known to very few. On the verge of the Arno and visible from Pino's front windows was a miserable little tree which somehow managed to retain a few withered leaves until late in December. Norman's belief was that if a few leaves or even one leaf remained on the tree at midnight of December 31st that would be a good omen for the coming year; but it would be a very bad omen if all were blown away. Apparently the end of one December was a particularly anxious time, as a heavy gale blew up. In those days, with an unrealised hope that they might drink less, Pinorman put their chairs at the window end of the *salone* to watch the tree, and set the flask of Chianti in the scullery at the farthest end of the flat. They called it *il sorge*, the source or fountain; and when their glasses were empty they would say "*Andiamo al sorge*," and back they would go, arm-in-arm, fill glasses, and then anxiously return to watch the last sere leaves fluttering in the gale.

Then he had the universal "Salute!" or "Gesundheit" when somebody sneezed. He beat his spectacles-case whenever he lost and eventually recovered it, as he frequently did, in order to punish it and warn it not to disappear again. He liked to keep up such childhood beliefs as the Tazzelwurm and Pino's "Voolley-Voolley"— by 'Pino's' I mean that Pino had enthusiastically adopted it. I used to think that all this was fun, but Pino demurred— "My dear boy, you do not know how superstitious is Norman." It may be so. I think he was a little worried about that sixty-third year.

Laudator temporis acti he was, but then what old man isn't? There was a time when the younger Athenians got so sick of boasters about Marathon that they would have liked to wring the necks of the survivors. Like Reggie, Norman chose to think that he belonged to an apex of humanity, whereafter there was only decline. True, he did not boast of his wit and sparkle, but deplored the woolliness and languor of his juniors, their lack of zest, the singular fact (unregistered by other physiologists) that their blood was two degrees below normal. Observe his dedication to his juvenile fellow-traveller, the enigmatic Eric: "I am convinced we had more fun." So what was he grumbling about? Obviously, I know nothing about the behaviour of the gentlemen of Tilquhillie, Karlsruhe and Piccadilly in years before I was born. Much may be laid to epoch. The Douglases and George Moores and Arthur Symonses and Reggie Turners braced the moral fibre and contracted a stern zest for high deeds by their repeated and gallant stormings of the approaches to the Burlington Arcade and the box-offices of London Music Halls, whereas their futile and sub-normal juniors frittered away their youth and any virility they may have had in Artois and Picardy, Ypres and the Somme, Salonika and Gallipoli and Gaza and on monotonous ocean voyages and marine bickerings. Let us gratefully recognise our superiors.

I think it no accident that the years 1928-32, when Norman began to realise that he was 'written out' in the higher levels of his mind, were also years of much publishing activity. He hoped to make enough money to provide for his old age. However bored he might be, he desperately wanted to go on living. I have a memory—a vignette—of the railway station at Florence (1937 therefore, because otherwise I left by car) and Norman and Pino there to see us off. Norman takes me aside and urgently reminds me that I have promised to let him know at once if I find in the scientific periodicals I read any 'means of prolonging life'. I promise, wondering why anyone wants to go on living after youth has fled.

I think those 1928-32 books were a desperate effort to earn enough money to buy himself an annuity for the barren and dismal years ahead. For my part I think that *Looking Back* and *How About Europe?* do not show any perceptible intellectual decline. Both have excellent passages, yet both read like 'made' books, built of unrelated fragments somehow glued together, and both full of echoes. Is there perhaps a loss of power in them? I shall not enquire too closely.

Now, according to Pino, Norman did succeed in making enough money to buy an annuity sufficient for an *homme seul* of simple tastes pre-1939. Every time he got a few hundreds or so from a book he was able to increase the annuity. Whether this was true or not I cannot say, but it certainly explains Norman's methods of publication. He realised that he was not and could not be a popular author, but that he had a real asset in his standing as a collector's author. So, with Scottish intelligence and eye to the main chance, he worked out his system of himself publishing a first limited edition to scoop up the profits of the collector's market, and then selling the copyright of the

library and cheap editions for what he could get in a lump
sum. In those days such a transaction was free of taxation
—authors had not then benefited by Anglo-American fiscal
encouragement of their art on a scale which leaves Leo X
and Louis XIV in the ranks of mere pauperisers. In *Late
Harvest* Norman represents one or two of these transactions
as a public service. The books and papers used for *How
About Europe?* cost him, he says importantly and with
anguish, no less than thirty-five pounds. The 100 copies
of his subscribers' edition of *Capri Materials* cost so much
to produce that (I weep for Adonais) he and Pino cleared
only thirty pounds between them. No doubt both these
statements are perfectly true. And yet he must have made
much more than thirty-five pounds out of *How About
Europe?*, while he omits to mention the 500 copies of *Capri
Materials* at thirty shillings which were very cheaply
knocked off from the type of the subscribers' edition.
On top of these works the period 1928–32 includes the
compilation of obscene *Limericks*, put forth possibly to
discredit *Lady Chatterley's Lover* as an obscene publication—
of course to make a little honest money also—*Nerinda* (old
stuff), *One Day*, the Bavarian Frog and Lizard article, and
even the reprint of *The Angel of Manfredonia*. And why not?
Why shouldn't Norman Douglas have a few pounds a week?

According to Pino—and I repeat "according to Pino"—
they worked out an ingenious method of disposing of
some of the unsold stock of the Lungarno Series. After
dinner they would retire to Pino's flat, open another
flask, and "Norman put on disc and dance about and is very
happy." Then he would write in unsold copies some of his
pungent and witty dedications to real or imaginary friends,
the real ones of course being defunct. Whereupon Pino,
moving from the status of dearest friend to second-hand
book-seller, would send them to the London book sales,

with a reserve price. Pino said they did pretty well, and certainly Norman's fine-old-Scottish-gentleman's protest against people who sold his letters seems to support rather than invalidate Pino's artless tale. I most heartily hope Norman made enough to buy a decent annuity. If he did, the tales of his 'starving' on Capri seem a little sensational; and I suspect they were sales-talk with a view to getting a handsome advance on his *Venus in the Kitchen*. Incidentally, the obituary sneers at his poverty came unhandsomely from people who had been more ready to pirate than to pay him.

In those years when he was no longer at the top of his form it was surely natural that he preferred to meet other people over a meal or the after-dinner flask. In any case that was the natural hour of society for one of his convivial nature, and he had long before rid himself of the exigencies of ordinary social intercourse—the tea parties and the cocktail parties and all the rest of the silly waste of time. Yet, in spite of this bohemianism, he retained as long as I was seeing him (up till 1938) certain manners which showed that he had lived among ceremonious people. He had the diplomatic bow from the chair, the scarcely perceptible but real lifting of the hams from the seat, accompanied by the courteous inclination of the head and trunk. It was but a few weeks back that I received such a bow from a French diplomat, and it went to my heart like a dagger of regret—Norman!

The miserable losses of old age, with the fact that his sons had their way to make in the world, caused him to cling very closely to Pino, and made him jealous of those who had some share of Pino's rather exigent regard. His jealousy of Reggie was clear to us all, and he would have felt much the same about Charles (whom Pino loved) but for the fact that his profession kept him in London and his hobbies took him to Greece. It had never occurred to me that Norman might have been jealous even of me, until I read his edition of Pino's *Moving Along* and saw how childishly he had cut out all the things about our trips Pino had so often said he meant to put into the book. I find much more difficulty in forgiving him for working on Pino's instable will so that he seemed to betray Lawrence, for whom in 1930 and thereabouts Pino had a genuine (I hope) and certainly profitable devotion. Whatever Norman's camp followers may say, there are a few of us (Frieda and Frere and I among them) who know that what Pino is made to say against Lawrence in *Memoirs of a Bookseller* is not true in substance or in fact, and is a repudiation of all that Pino professed in those years of his devotion to Lawrence and his memory. As I have before mentioned, Pino was so enthusiastic that he used to talk of trying to get permission from the Italian authorities to put up a laudatory inscription on the pine tree in whose shade Lawrence wrote *Lady Chatterley's Lover*. Would he have dreamed of doing such a thing if he had thought about Lawrence the disagreeable and disparaging thoughts Norman wrote into Pino's books?

All the same, I dare say that under his exterior cynicism and unscrupulousness Norman had or hid a capacity for affection. I think he was really devoted to his sons, and that since life so often deprived him of their companionship he made Pino something like a substitute son. If in the preceding pages I have given the impression that Pino was in any sense his butt, that is due to my clumsy reporting. He was not. Of course Norman enjoyed the Arlecchino in him, and the Boccacio junior who had such stores of vitality and laughter. He kept Norman alive. . . .

And now I am in the mood to imitate Norman himself at the end of *Looking Back*, and to cut short these recollections abruptly. I have said most of what I remember and have given that future biographer most of the information which otherwise will die with me—he is welcome to take or reject as he chooses. In these pages I have gossiped about three men, and to me Charles comes first, then Pino, and only after them Norman. I thought to end this book with one of Charles's latest letters of 1948, but I cannot find one which does not in its kindness over-praise me, so that if I published it I might be misunderstood. What shall I say of him, except—disregarding quantity—*Non sum qualis eram boni sub regno Caroli*? Here is a paragraph from one of his later letters which prepared me for his flight from an England where men such as he were no longer wanted or esteemed.

"I am very sorry I have been so feeble a correspondent. I have been v. mouldy ever since coming back from France last autumn. I've had a new doctor from Truro, and he seems to be doing more good than the first. He says: Get off, into sun. So we are going, to Kenya, if it can be fixed up for next month. Thank you for your remarks on Jamaica. Three weeks ago I went to Dorset, and L. to London. There she saw a Business-Man, who carolled of the Caribbean—and she was instantly persuaded you were right. He loved it all. Kenya no doubt is full of governmental and military horrors. But there is coffee to drink; ladies'-finger bananas; paw-paws; the most marvellous scenery and animal views; a handleable range of climate; no Afrikaans. For a visit. We shan't make preparations for an exodus, as we foolishly put on the probability list for South Africa last year . . ."

Not long afterwards he died suddenly of heart failure in Kenya. He was the least selfish man I have ever known, as . . . but I will not complete the sentence.

INDEX

214